INTERNAL KAI

MW00637368

Mind Matters &
The Seven Gates of Power

By Hayashi Tomio

Wind School
Convent Station, New Jersey

Copyright © 2014 Christopher J. Goedecke

All rights reserved
including the right of reproduction
in whole or in part in any form

ISBN 978-0-9792697-4-5

Published by Wind School
16 Braidburn Way
Convent Station, New Jersey 07960

Book Design by Kathleen Otis

Printed In the United States of America

"Do not go where the path may lead.
Go instead to where there is no path and leave a trail."

R. W. Emmerson

PERSONAL NOTE

The Martial Ways discussed in this book step off the path of those media-hyped disciplines that focus solely on physical, competitive, or self-defense objectives.

This book broadly addresses other vital aspects of the Asian martial lineage traditions whose goal is to awaken the whole person for transforming and transcending all manner of conflict.

Just as the act of walking does not define the totality of human life—kicking, punching, shouting, and getting our opponent's to cry 'uncle', does not define the totality of the Martial Ways. Though these actions represent its outer objectives there also awaits every seeker a seldom explored, rich, subjective, inner tradition. We must not forget that all our Martial institutions once sprang from the wisdom that resides within.

The ideas presented in this book are available to all people, not just students of the Asian Fighting arts, and although these ideas will require some effort to put into practical use, the greatest personal satisfaction and accomplishment always comes from deliberate endeavor.

If only one person is willing to journey into these far fields, the heart of the 'Inner Way' is sure to keep beating.

CONTENTS

CONTENTS

INTRODUCTION

HAJIME!

Begin

From the moment I had set about writing *The Soul Polisher's Apprentice* in 2007, a book that intimately explored the philosophical and spiritual nature of martial training by real people, I knew I would eventually undertake this project on internal *karatedo* practices - a richly intoxicating, but daunting subject. Given the masters who would have much to say in this regard, I felt that same nervous twinge that a novice performer might feel facing a panel of stoic-faced judges. I would be

putting myself on the line, hoping for a favorable response. Obviously, my determination to press forward succeeded. I'd like to thank a former student, named Lynn, who unwittingly tilted the scales in favor of my presenting this subject in book format to the general martial art community.

While conducting a belt test one evening, I had asked Lynn if she would perform her *seisan kata* (a traditional seventy-move, Okinawan solo floor pattern). Despite feeling acutely nervous, she thanked me, "For the manner in which you asked me to perform," she stated. "Because you did not say come out and demonstrate the *ideal* or *perfect* kata, or the *dojo's* kata, or the *isshin* kata, but asked me instead to perform *my* kata, you allowed me to be totally myself."

The best any martial teacher can ask of a student is to move honestly and authentically. In this light, I present a book about *my* Internal karatedo practices in regards to their subtle, sometimes hidden technical arrangements or components. It may not be the classical *Chinese* way, or the *Japanese or Okinawan* understanding, or old *master so and so-so's* lesson. It's simply *my* way. I don't lay any claim that this way is better than anyone else's. I can say that my discoveries have greatly benefited me personally, as well as many of my advanced students, and I think that our experiences and descriptions can offer open-minded readers opportunities into their own untapped martial potential. I also want to express my gratitude for all those who guided me high enough up the martial ladder to see what had previously been obscured from my vision.

Ultimately, the meaning of any martial art is about its relevancy and value to our present and personal lives, regardless of its previous historical merits. This book is about my personal experiences, about the insights that I, and others in my organization, have observed about a covert nature to martial technique and its underlying principles. We believe these principles, readily verified by both lay and martial individuals, remain concealed to most modern day practitioners.

1998, Tian Zhua, a senior, thirty-year practitioner in our school, asked me if I had been recording my findings. I took his hint to create a "brain annex," the apt term for the notebook another of my *yudansha* used for everything he couldn't fit into his head. I started electronically journaling in May of that year. Since then, I have compiled nearly one thousand pages of observations regarding an aspect of martial study that had been veiled from me for over two decades—and I considered myself an astute practitioner. All that journaling saved me a great deal of time in structuring and distilling the material that follows.

Like the ever-faithful disciple, whenever my teachers pointed the way, I dutifully locked my eyes on

the goal of bettering myself, until I had no teacher. That's when I took a deep look inward and hit the *Do*, big time.

At this moment I am a professional sensei entering my forty-fifth year of training. I have devoted four precious decades of my life teaching martial arts full-time, six days a week. As the years passed I found myself gravitating away from the mainstream sportification of the Martial Ways, instead intuitively taking a gentle fork in the road toward inner or internal study or, what Okinawan stylists refer to as the *Michi* (Do). Internal practice better suits my sensitive temperament. I am a focused teacher, continuously looking for ways to enhance lessons for my student body. This disposition has allowed me to mold critical ideas into palatable lessons.

In an effort to compliment my personal observations derived through many trial and error experiments over a twenty-two year period, I also sought writings that confirmed or challenged my findings. I found the greatest accord in the fundamentals of internal work, but the technical expressions varied greatly amongst the world's internal fighting systems. No doubt, such variants explain the many family *ryu* or specialized systems worldwide that to this day still maintain themselves under a cloak of protective or proprietary secrecy. There are internal systems that advocate no physical forms work at all to those with highly complex and lengthy external movement patterns. I frequently encounter obtuse language, or confusing over-generalizations for the use of the terms *Chi* or *Ki* amongst many in the Hard-style community who bandy this term about without a firm foothold on its workings. This book will also consider the perspective of those experts who do not ascribe any paranormal or hidden skills to the martial arts outside of external talents and a primed physiology, or to use their common label, proper 'structure.'

Such diversity of opinions and the personal experiences behind them made me curious about the universal truths we would encounter if we stripped away all the invested egos and the "house language" of our various *ryu* or systems. I consider the primary functions of an effective teacher the ability to break down a subject matter into easily assimilated lessons, and to make them downright savory and compelling to our students—which I hope to accomplish here.

Magic Eyes: A Martial Enigma

I confronted a martial enigma twenty-two years into my teaching career that left me incredulous. The dictionary describes an *enigma* as a mysterious, puzzling or difficult thing to understand. How could

I have missed something so significant? How could it be that with all my training, all my teaching experiences, all my reading and thinking about the martial arts, that I had been blind to half of its essential nature? This was truly a riddle of epic proportions.

Strangely, as I looked around, I found that I was not alone. Many of the professional martial artists I have encountered over the last two decades also had, and still have, little idea about this missing dimension. Entering into dialog with martial artists on this subject yielded a wide gamut of responses ranging from genuine awe and avid curiosity to stone cold silence, arrogance, rudeness, even outright denial that there is any more to martial arts than what met *their* eyes.

As I stated in *The Soul Polisher's Apprentice* (Wind School), no matter how big your tractor or how much horsepower, or how many miles you have logged, you cannot plow a field that you do not know exists. A huge field of information exists embedded in the heart of most traditional Hard style kata. But we need a pair of magic eyes to see it.

In 1979 Christopher Tyler invented a way to create a stunning visual image *within an image*. It was called a *stereogram*. Interestingly, the embedded second image only becomes visible by averting your eyes directly from the primary one. When I first looked at what is now called a 'Magic Eye' image I couldn't see any hidden picture. After minutes of hard staring and some doubt there really was a second picture, I relaxed my gaze and it strikingly loomed up like a turtle emerging from murky water. This same phenomenon occurred regarding my experiences with internal martial arts. I never saw it in my surface practice. Then one day, unexpectedly, it loomed large. Consider this work a finger pointing toward this amazing horizon. Be patient. Relax your gaze. If you see what I did, you will be hard pressed to deny its reality or importance to your martial art.

Inklings of Change

I began formal martial training at age seventeen in the Fall of 1968 at a large pioneering suburban karate dojo in New Jersey, informally known as the Bank Street School. I trained in what I would have once confidently labeled a 'Hard style' martial art—Okinawan Karate's, Isshin Ryu. I've since learned that the great Chinese internal systems like *Tai Chi, Hsing Yi, Ba Gua* or the more esoteric system of Water Boxing (*Liu He Ba Fa*), don't hold the exclusive rights to soft-style insights and principles. Under the thick skin of many Western-adopted karate systems, particularly traditional kata-based arts with movement patterns created prior to the Industrial Revolution, there lies the

little-explored technical, psychological, and spiritual field of **Internal** karate. In China this study was known as *Quan* or *Chuan Fa*–named for its Buddhist influence. The Japanese called this multi-dimensional art *Kempo*.

Something's Missing

My internal practices did not begin until 1991, twenty-six years later, and well into a successful career as a sensei of Okinawan karate. I was teaching a large active student body when a single event awoke me to the profound inner character of my technical practices. This event happened purely by coincidence and it involved one of my senior practitioners, a Korean War veteran and dedicated karateka, sensei Joe Noonan. Having previously spent a year's work on pressure point theory and practice, Joe and I decided to shift our curiosities to the principles underlying pressure point strikes. This decision proved such a major turning point in my career that it took us on a twenty-three year quest to determine how the human Subtle Energy Body enhanced not only martial technique but also our everyday actions. We plunged headlong into the mystery of power with the martial art of Isshinryu as our guide.

Mysterious Incident

One evening sensei Joe Noonan and I were practicing small circle wrist releases, a staple in many dojos. In a typical exchange, Joe would firmly hold my wrist as I rehearsed rotating my arm in tight clockwise or counter-clockwise circles to break his grip. During one escape it seemed as if Joe wasn't holding me at all. In fact, my escape felt ridiculously effortless. I hadn't used any pressure point strikes as a prior set up. We were both seasoned, senior *Doka* (Way student) with firm grip strengths and conditioned arms. Why had this particular escape felt so easy?

We had no idea that we had just crossed a mighty perceptual threshold from 'Hard style' into 'Soft style' principles. We had entered the sacred chamber of power, the playground of the masters—Internal Energy. The universe had graciously swung open a hallowed temple door. Like curious boys we dove headfirst into our newfound treasure room. From that moment forward we knew, instantly, and unmistakably, that something vital had been missing from our curriculum and from the curriculums of thousands of martial practitioners around the world. Admittedly, we were latecomers to the internal experience but as the Roman historian, Titus Livius, stated, *"better late than never."*

11

The West Coast, internal master, Bruce Frantzis has amply described the effects of internal technique as *"cutting like a hot knife through butter."* That day my arm, sizzling with Qi, seared thru sensei Noonan's grip. But more importantly, it sheared the thick mental block that had prevented the two of us from previously seeing an amazing dimension of human power.

Looking back, I now understand that it's not unusual for a serendipitous act to spark a critical insight. You might recall an event where your own actions were disproportionate to the result, like having your training partner surprisingly felled by your accidental, *effortless* back kick or palm strike. Suddenly, you awakened to 'real' power.

Around the time of this fortuitous incident, I had been instructing a core of advanced students in the esoteric *Sanchin* kata – a form whose fundamental principles trace back generations to China's Shaolin Temple (ShorinJi, Jap.) at the time of the legendary monk, Bodhidharma. In addition to our dabbling for months in pressure point work, Joe and his wife had been practicing *chi kung*. This mixture of advanced kata practice, standing grappling escapes, point work, and chi kung exercise created the perfect training stew that sparked an evolution in our technique.

Relying heavily on our intuitions, we chased the mystery of the effortless wrist release, sure that if we could capture its rational we'd be onto something big. We were not disappointed. New informational doorways swung open so fast that our heads swam with consistent and unbelievable break-

throughs week after week. Looking back, my diary notations took on a meandering quality as Joe and I, and later additional advanced *yudansha* (black belts), followed our natural curiosities as one might kayak a winding river. Whenever we got stumped we'd place our theories on the back burner and work our way around peripheral issues until we nailed the sought after rationale.

The insights continue to this day. I even joked one night with Joe, while pointing to my pastel painting of Isshinryu Karate's founder, Tatsuo Shimabuku, that the old master must be rolling in his grave at our findings.

This book will touch upon the most important and consistent features we discovered since that day in 1992 and that we now use in our advanced training. This book is also my personal accounting about the nature of internal and external martial practice.

My goal is to broaden reader's understanding of the 'Do' component in the Martial Ways regardless of the style or system practiced, and also to bridge what I see is a broad gap of technical understanding between the Hard and Soft styles. This work is also an attempt to activate a dynamic *skeleton in the kata* closet. For very strong evidence consistently points to internal principles embedded in all Japanese, Okinawan, and Tae Kwon Do Forms. This is a book therefore, for people who would like to engage a 'great room' of Soft principles embedded within their Hard style disciplines, for those who are curious about the larger paths within the Martial Ways, and for those seeking better tools to cope with their everyday conflicts whether on the inside or outside of their skin, or their training halls.

Internal practice has powerfully enhanced my martial study. It has increased my physical skills, added a renewed vitality and exciting dimensionality to my art, my martial organization, and my overall relationships in life. I hope this information provides readers with a springboard for a more penetrating grasp of their own disciplines, opens up more dialog on the subject, or at least offers a tantalizing contrast to one's current or future study.

The book is divided into five sections: **Part 1** revisits why we train in martial arts and address its core nature. **Part 2** looks at how the brain/mind is intimately entwined with our physical practices. **Part 3** explores 'Warrior Power' with a seven-tiered template of the distinct ways in which we *all* use our personal powers. **Part 4** discusses the working fundamentals of the *Subtle Energy Body*. **Part 5** invites us into a dialog amongst ten senior karateka and takes a brief, practical look at some of the internal components of three common martial techniques.

THE MYSTERY OF POWER

Everyday, all around us, ordinary people are experiencing extraordinary powers in ways that defy mainstream and even scientific comprehension. The great attraction for the martial arts often comes from the tremendous physical energy they unleash. But in addition to imparting practical skills, the Martial Ways have also been linked to some mystifying phenomenon. For thousands of years paranormal events have been equated to the Asian body/mind masters. They recognized that *extra*-ordinary abilities were a consequence of diligent, mindful training. On a whim, I solicited my immediate dojo student body, friends, and martial alliances for personal stories of any unusual powers

or unexplainable events they might have experienced on or off the mat. They had a lot to say. All of the contributors are normal, intelligent, psychologically-grounded individuals. Here are twenty-three tales, including several from my own direct experiences, illustrating how unusual and/or unexplainable events occur around us all the time.

Lights Out!

"Nine of us in the acupuncture school had been taking Qi Gong with David for about eight weeks," explained Roberto, an advanced karate practitioner and second year acupuncture student. This day, his professor, David Miller, had a surprise for the class. "After two full hours of training he took out twelve candles," Roberto continued. "We thought he was going to lead us into a meditation. Instead, he struck a match, lit every candle, and placed them on the desk at the front of the classroom. He said, "Today, you will extinguish candles with Qi." Some students were naturally skeptical. The rest of us (including me) got goose bumps from the anticipation. David backed away six or seven feet from the candles. Then, with only a flick of his wrist, one candle went out. Someone asked, "Aren't you just flicking air to put it out?" "Well, okay," David replied. He stepped back further, perhaps ten feet from the candle, and had the student hold his hand up to it to feel for any wind. After he confirmed that there wasn't any wind coming from his wrist motion, David flicked his wrist again. The candle went out. The flame didn't flicker like when you blow out birthday candles. It just dispersed and went out. The same skeptical student was still unsatisfied, so David asked for an acupuncture needle. Standing about three to four feet away from the candle, he plainly and calmly, without rushing, without flicking, simply turned his wrist over and pointed the needle at the candle. The flame went out in the same dispersing manner. David remarked afterward, "With a little practice all of you can do this." We spilled a lot of wax on the floor that night.

Dragonback

A career Kempo instructor related this tale: "One evening filled with stories of martial prowess over a couple of beers, a mutual friend and devoted Ba Gua student named Brad, asked if I had ever heard of the *Dragonback*. I hadn't, but I was ready for a new experience. I asked him to demonstrate. When he glanced behind me for a suitable landing strip I knew I was in trouble. I had a strong enough background in break falling to know that tensing on impact would be bad, so I relaxed. Brad then

16

casually laid his hands upon my shoulders and said, "I'm going to take a few breaths to organize myself then I am going to push you."

As I wondered how I would react to his 'Dragonback', he said, "I'm ready." WHAM! I was skidding backward on the seat of my pants before my ears had registered his sharp exhale. Brad's feet remained side by side just outside shoulder width. His arms hovered loosely in the air. I recall sensing a subtle undulation of energy rising up through his body sending a shockwave down his arms and into his palms lying lightly on my shoulders. I was literally *floored*!

The Flute In The Box

I was sharing my perspective on transcendental practices with an East Coast interior designer and *Feng Shui* consultant named Kim, whose son was an advanced student in our school, when I found myself eager to muscle test her to demonstrate a point. We stepped over to what is known in Feng Shui as a *piercing arrow*, a right-angled, jutting corner wall. "Under most normal circumstances any person standing by a piercing arrow should experience a physical weakening," I told her. Yet when Kim stood by the piercing arrow in her foyer, oddly she tested the opposite—strong.

Unbeknownst to me, Kim had purchased a flute two weeks prior from the Yun Lin Buddhist Temple in Berkeley, California to use as a Feng Shui cure in her practice. She believed that a flute purchased from Professor Lin, the late head of the Black Hat Sect of Feng Shui, would be "spiritually active". She had forgotten placing the triangular, Fed Ex box containing the flute along the corner of the foyer where we both stood. The presence of the flute had negated the poison arrow's energy, for when we moved the flute, she tested, just as I had anticipated—weak. Kim's intuition was right. She experienced the results first hand. The vibrant energy of the flute had permeated the space around it.

The $2.7 Million Dollar Home

Vicky, the realtor, had tried unsuccessfully to sell her client's house for over a year. Thinking outside of the box, she enrolled in a Feng Shui course and asked Kim, the course facilitator, if she would consult with the husband and wife clients. Kim agreed. She walked thru the house, noted its atrocious design, and discovered the wife was still emotionally attached to her home. The couple agreed to a 'transcendental cure' to release the energies that bound them to the property. Two and a half weeks later the house sold just twenty thousand dollars shy of the full asking price.

Touch Down!

Life events had taken Jay's finances in the wrong direction. At this low point Jay had received a CD gift called "The Awakening" from his sensei. At first Jay thought the CD's new-age message was in his words, "a bogus piece of crap." Nevertheless, he listened to it. The CD's message told him that he could attract whatever he wanted into his life. So he decided to experiment on the CD's two most powerful laws: The Law of Attraction and the Law of Deliberate Creation. He had planned to attend a 2008 Super Bowl Sunday party hosted by his new boss the following day. The Giants were playing the Patriots and there would be gambling at the party. So he spent an hour prepping his mind by visualizing himself winning the gambling pool. He wrote out and spoke aloud that he would win. When he arrived at the party he noted the different gambling boards set up. Not really a football fan, Jay simply decided to spread a $250 dollar wager on various boards. Surprisingly, he won the first quarter. Though the Patriots had been favored, the Giants had grabbed victory in the last thirty seconds. At the end of the game came an announcement. Jay had won the entire $3,000 grand prize. At that time he really needed the money. Jay attributed his winnings to the message on the CD. After that success he made another note to himself to earn $10,000. Two weeks later he closed a business deal for $7,000. On a successful streak, Jay focused next on earning $100,000. Shortly thereafter, he earned a commission of $70,000. The last we spoke he was focusing on attracting $1,500,000!

Stop Me If You Can!

I hosted a Buddhist martial arts master from Tennessee for a five-day seminar in 2000. On the last day of the monk's visit I asked him to step into my private dojo to share some advanced kempo techniques. Instead, he insisted that I grab his chambered right hand and try to stop him from extending his arm. I gripped his wrist tightly with both my hands and assumed a strong stance. The monk commented that no matter how big a person was or how hard he gripped, no one could stop him from extending his arm. With that said, he thrust his right arm forward and hurled me backward many feet.

I asked if he would repeat his punch one more time. He agreed. This time I gripped his wrist with a single hand, though he insisted I hold with both. After I stated one hand will do just fine, the monk thrust his arm forward again. To his utter dismay he couldn't get it out of the chamber.

"What are you doing?" he asked incredulously. I answered, "That is what I've been trying to show you all week!"

Backfist Voodoo

Laura, a middle-aged, intermediate-ranked karate student shared her Thursday morning private sessions with two other women. Her lesson focused on backfist strikes against a free-standing heavy bag. Laura relished the intense physical outlet of her karate practice. When her instructor inquired about her spunk, Laura half-jokingly blurted out that she pictured her boss's face each time she struck the bag. When she later described her boss, a local parish administrator at the town church, insensitive to everyone around him, her teacher remarked, "Be careful what you project. Your boss has probably developed a rash all over his face." Laura's jaw dropped. Her employer had indeed recently developed a mysterious skin condition over his entire face – a fact that her sensei could not possibly have known.

Zapped!

The Tennessee-based Buddhist monk, Tenshin Arakawa, related the following story:

"I was teaching a seminar to a whole bunch of 18-26 year old, half-aikido, half-kyusho, wet behind the ears, Wadoryu shodans. Their sensei was ex-military, early sixties, CIA, pictures with the president, green beret, with a little dojo of 60-80 students in the middle of nowhere. After the seminar this sensei invited me to his school. He wanted me to demonstrate some pressure point work. He explained that he was not really skeptical, just do this favor for him. I explained that I didn't test pressure points on women, children, or the elderly. I'm 5'9". He was maybe 6'1". I told him I'd give him a little *zap*. He would feel a jolt. He actually turned out to be a highly reactive subject. His legs buckled. I had to use revival points to re-stimulate him. Afterward, over lunch, he asked me to demonstrate on one of his students, a humble brown belt, weightlifter. I mentioned that avid weightlifting brings the arteries to the surface—more subcutaneous than inter-muscular, making my strikes particularly effective. I demonstrated the move with great precision. The student's eyes rolled back into his head. He fell to the ground. I had to revive him. His sensei was so impressed that he wanted me to teach all his brown and black belts. Next, he begged me to show him something really good. I agreed, but I also told him my technique would be an illusion. I told him that I would touch, excite, one point and that tonight or tomorrow he would urinate some blood on and off. He wouldn't need a doctor and he was not to worry, he wouldn't bleed to death. On the third or fourth day his bleeding would stop completely. With that said, I hit him. Sure enough, the next day, he urinated

blood. He tried calling me for reassurance but I wasn't around. He became frightened and went to his doctor who charged him a small fortune for medical tests but could not figure what was wrong. He was so serious when he saw me again. I told him the process was an illusion. I was just fooling with the unknown."

Switching Lanes

Eric's black Audi sped down the fast lane of a dark and rain-soaked Highway 287, heading home. Few cars were on the road that night. Visibility was poor. Eric always drove in the left lane but, as he described it, "Some inner voice told me to shift to the middle lane." He couldn't remember why he should shift, simply that it felt imperative. Less than a minute later, now in the middle lane, he sped past the burnt out hulk of a car, dead still in the left lane, its rear light reflectors smashed. Eric would have been instantly killed had he stayed in the left lane. There was no way that he would have seen the wreck. His mysterious intuition to switch lanes in the middle of the night had avoided a head-on collision with a disabled car.

The Christmas Cactus

Eric's twenty-year old Christmas cactus plant bloomed twice a year. But when he entered a shaky, two-year marriage that ended in divorce, the plant ceased flowering for the next fifteen years. Then, Eric experienced a traumatic event while taking his test for Black Belt. During a heated *kumite* (sparring match) he broke his tibula and fibia completely in half. Though it was a ghastly tragedy, it caused profound and surprisingly positive changes in his person. Coincidentally, his cactus suddenly re-bloomed and now flowers at least six times a year.

Gotta Go

Steve, a twenty-year martial art practitioner, recalls that he was once an ambitious college student tackling twenty-eight credits per semester and holding down three jobs. Living several states away gave him little time to visit his parents. But one weekend he felt an inexplicable desire to return home. His mother had left for the day to attend a Chinese Auction. His dad remained home alone. When Steve arrived at the family house he noticed a palor on his dad's face. "Indigestion," his father self-diagnosed and disappeared into the bathroom. Sensing something ominous, Steve called

an ambulance, despite his father's protests. Doctors found that Steve's father was having a heart attack. He probably would have died that day had his son not had an inexplicable urge to visit for the weekend. Was his visit a coincidence or did Steve pick up on a subtle energy communication?

Unexpected Reaction

Sometimes we forget how disorienting a simple, unexpected action can be. Nick, an active Kempo student, had such an experience while visiting his brother-in-law, Sal. Sal was a stocky, street-savvy recruit at the police academy in upstate New York learning how to handle perpetrators. One day he was explaining to Nick how the police managed difficult street encounters. In his surprise demo, Sal snatched Nick's arm. Instead of naturally pulling back to resist Sal's clutch, Nick thrust his hand forward, disorienting Sal who nearly lost his balance. Sal was sure Nick would *resist* his pull. Sal's confidence drained right out of his face. His attempt to dominate the situation had been completely thwarted by Nick's unexpected reaction.

Dreamcatcher

The day after Halloween, 2008, I awoke from an unsettling dream about a former student whom I had not seen for several years. I had dreamed that she was in a dispute with an aggressive, older male standing under a bridge over a stream. I felt compelled to contact her because of the disturbing imagery of her potential rape. I emailed my dream to her. Two days later she sent this response: "So great to hear from you... it has been awhile since we have seen each other but details may have to wait.... I am eager to address the dream you had...your dream gave me goose bumps...because of its accuracy... Halloween night I went out with a male work friend after our shift ended, we are just friends, I want nothing more with him, we were having such a good time but then after too much to drink he kept trying to hook up with me and I had to push him away like a hundred times. It was annoying and a little weird that he kept trying and I remember thinking this guy seems like some-one who may not understand that *no* means *no*. He is young and immature so I brushed it off and handled it, but the idea of rape came into my head, and even the day after still the same thoughts and my gut said to be careful around this guy. I got your email a day or two after. The other thing about your dream that is accurate is that I live in apartment ... at the base of a huge and an beautiful park, across the street is a view of bridge over a large pond."

Omens

Many students have recounted to me martial art dreams relating to their evolving physical powers or lack thereof. Some of these dreams have proven quite prophetic. The graphic designer for this book, Kathy, whose husband is a black belt, related the following story:

In 1978 I was sitting in a restaurant with a friend when I had an overwhelming and foreboding sense of my mother. I immediately called her to see if she was all right. She was fine. A week later, I had a strange dream in which a burglar entered my house through my living room window and grabbed me. I've never been grabbed by anyone in my dreams. I've always managed to escape. In retrospect, I felt the burglar in my dream represented the Angel of Death coming for my mother because she died two weeks later, on Friday the 13th. Even stranger, shortly after my dream, a burglar actually broke in to my home and stole my jewelry. He came in through the same living room window.

Jump!

A beginning kempo student named Konstantin shared an old family story about his uncle, Michale, who lived in the central Asian country of Kyrgyzstan. Konstantin described his teenage uncle, "of average height and not very athletic." One day, while taking a walk, Michale was attacked by a large, vicious dog. Fearing serious injury, he bolted with the dog in pursuit. Rounding a bend, Michael found himself penned in by a two-meter high concrete construction wall. The next thing he remembers is standing atop its slender ledge perfectly balanced with the canine frothing below. In one leap Michael had landed feet first atop a six-foot high wall! Did adrenaline alone give Micheal extraordinary jumping abilities?

Supersize Me!

An Emergency Room nurse, named Chris, who worked at a large suburban New Jersey hospital, decided to pursue his post black belt studies with me after graduating college. I had him focus upon the esoteric, Okinawan Sanchin Kata. In one class, while standing about five feet apart, I asked him to note of our size differences. Chris stood 5'10". I stand 6'4". After Chris had performed three sanchin katas we stood across from one another again. Chris noticed that he appeared to have grown considerably larger. This bizarre phenomenon occurs every time he performs Sanchin.

Grand Slam

For two decades Mr. K, an avid martial artist and award winning Physical Education teacher, had played on his local softball league. After black belt he learned internal energy principles and believed they could enhance his batting skills. For months he worked on postural adjustments to his batting. "It seemed so simple," he later reflected. "All I did was place my top hand on the bat and move my thumb from the traditional grip to an Okinawan style punch position. I also made sure that my hands were relaxed. Just before contacting the ball, I'd tighten my bottom hand. I think my power was derived from tightening my top hand with the thumb action. I would breathe out just before contact and push my energy down into my gut. I believe all these factors contributed to my hitting the ball harder and farther than I have ever hit it. I surprised many an infielder with blistering grounders and line drives. Even the outfielders were amazed when they saw the ball sailing over their heads. Needless to say, there isn't a day that goes by now that I don't use my chi to the max."

Wimp!

Mr. K added, "I still use my 'energy gating' for lifting heavy things. I've amazed many people who see me as a little guy, carrying very heavy objects. Yesterday, for example, I carried one forty-pound bag of fertilizer in each hand and draped a third bag over my arm. My bigger helper could only manage one bag—"wimp!"

TV Blooper

A Princeton University graduate and martial artist, Mike, in his forties, recalled a strange event during his teenage years. He and a friend had been watching TV one evening when he suddenly flew into what he called a "typical teenage rage" and found himself focusing all his anger at the center of the TV screen. POP! The TV screen flashed white then went totally black. Ever since, Mike has always had an eerie sense that his burst of anger had caused his TV's demise.

Shake, Rattle, And Roll

In July of 2007 I had the good fortune to learn a 1,000 year old, Tibetan energy cultivating form. The seventy-year old master who taught it to me stated that it was a high level internal exercise. I practiced it faithfully three times every day for one year. Of all the kata I have studied, this form caused

notable aftereffects. At the end of one session my limbs and torso began to shake in wildly ecstatic undulations for twenty unbroken minutes. My body *was moving me* without my conscious control! Chinese Chi Kung practitioners call this 'induced chi flow' where internal energy is stimulated to let loose in the body to open blocked channels.

Catch This!

Some years ago I attended a performance by a world famous mentalist known as 'The Amazing Kreskin'. A former student, who was a personal friend of Kreskin's, assured me that Kreskin's mental abilities were truly astonishing. So, when the opportunity presented itself I, along with several others, attended one of Kreskin's shows at a local museum. Three times during the performance Kreskin asked the audience to guess a number between one and one hundred. A very small group of us guessed correctly three consecutive times. Kreskin then asked me to stand up. I sat about fifteen rows back from the stage. He stepped off the stage, grabbed a very large note pad, and wrote something down. Turning to me, he yelled, "Tell me the first number that enters your head. NOW!"

As if a fireball had been thrown into my brain, the number 77 flashed in my mind. I yelled, "77." Kreskin turned his pad around so the audience could see that he had clearly written, in big bold print, number '77'.

Invisible Wall

Kate, a resident of Queensland Australia and a long term martial artist, related the following story:

"We had a visiting black belt from another club and I, who was basically a yellow belt at the time, was chosen to partner with him. We were doing attack/defenses, moving up and down the dojo floor in *zenkutsu dachi*. The last sequence required I do a downward block as a 'stop force with force' block against a front kick. *Ouch!*

The BB (black belt) who had a large powerful build charged me each time with full speed, full power. Before long my battered forearms were tender and swollen. After another length of the long dojo I was questioning the sense in continuing, as my arms were in a bad way, but I felt if I stopped this would show a lack of fighting spirit and that I'd be letting my sensei down in front of the visiting BB.

Finally I reached my limit. As his next kick came in hard and fast, I heard myself mentally scream

out "NO!" Though I hadn't made a physical sound, the BB reacted as though he'd slammed into a brick wall. His kick stopped short and he had to hop backwards on his supporting leg to regain his balance. On the next count, the same thing happened, only this time I don't think I mentally yelled anything. My sensei was watching from across the dojo and came up to see what was happening. He stood right next to us and counted again. The third time was just the same.

My sensei questioned the BB who said he didn't know what was happening. They examined the floor around us, and the bottom of the BB's feet. Not once did they look at me but I couldn't shake the conviction that in desperation I had projected an energy shield to protect myself. When they couldn't find anything to account for the episode, my sensei announced it was time to practice kata, for which I was vastly relieved."

Iron Palm

Ralph had spent three years developing his Iron Palm technique during his lengthy, thirty years of martial art training. One day he found himself in class getting lip from a young man who didn't think much about his skills, no less his Iron Palm strike. The guy brazenly challenged Ralph to strike him. Ralph hoped that a light tap would appease the situation. It didn't. Instead, realizing that Ralph's Iron Palm technique was ineffective he upped his condescending remarks and taunted further. Ralph hit him one more time, not any bit harder, except this time he filled his hand with chi. The kid ranted what a useless technique the Iron Palm strike was when suddenly he screamed and fell to the ground in full body seizure.

Who Cares?

Ralph tried unsuccessfully, each day, for months on end to break the patio block with his iron palm. The technique—hit with the flat of the palm from two inches above the block and don't use a lot of muscular force. One day, after sending chi into his hand, he hovered his palm inches over the patio block and effortlessly shattered it. He never duplicated the feat again but he had glimpsed that a part of himself which had stopped caring about the results had yielded the results.

PART ONE
WHY WE TRAIN

"What you live with, you learn; What you learn, you practice;
What you practice, you become; What you become has consequences!

Ritu Ghatourey

Why Martial Arts Were Created

We all have an innate desire to conquer the negativity in our lives, which is the cause of much human suffering. At the very least, we want a better grip on negotiating through life. Martial arts initially developed to help people in various world cultures evoke and evolve their warrior nature to implement effective and, we would like to believe, moral methods of self-protection in times of personal, and/or civil unrest. Martial training puts practical skills into the hands of individuals when and wherever the responsibility to protect themselves or loved ones falls squarely on their shoulders. As one comedic spin goes, "I carry martial arts because a cop is too heavy." But the martial arts, at their core, present both the study of and remedy for *many* levels of human-to-human conflicts. In the training hall this study begins with a candid look at our concerns about personal safety and also at our inadequacies, such as lack of coordination, flexibility, balance, strength, ill health or poor self-image, all the things that would prevent us from managing our safety. It then tackles head on, and specifically, the issues of actual or potential hostilities toward us.

In peaceful times the warrior arts were preserved and promoted through sport-competitions and public exhibitions. Such peacetime goals lift the bar of human potential and offer us a dynamic physical outlet. They build confidence and strengthen character, impart sound fitness principles while offering us resolutions for possible physical conflicts. Because the martial arts expand our options for behavior, they have also led many practitioners to an overall improvement in their quality of life. In Asia, when the martial arts intersected with Yogic, Buddhist and Taoist ideologies, they also morphed into an inner warriorhood to help people cope with intrapersonal imbalance and crisis as well. By refining the sensitivities through a consistent, organized, and ritualized training regime, one could obtain degrees of understanding and control over difficult life conditions and tap hidden storehouses of physical and mental strength. This less common martial journey is viewed as a spiritual or personal evolution. The full face of martial arts embraces both outer and inner wisdom and those who walk this path are called *Doka*, or Way followers.

Why We Don't All Practice Martial Arts
Although it would be a pragmatic skill for all ages, the idea of everyone achieving a Black Belt or

mastery of a martial art is unrealistic. We each have our own destinies to unlock and some of us do not require tapping this part of our nature to do so. Broad swaths of civilization also live in relative or at least manageable peacefulness. Secondly, most societies relegate the dirty work of self-protection to their law enforcement community. If they need emergency services, they rely on a squad car arriving in time. Third, an impressive number of obstacles prevent people from dipping freely into their personal well of warriorhood. To name a few; you may not believe such a well exists or is worth your time to explore. The authorities in your life; parents, older siblings, or mentors, may deny or demean its value. You may be too busy in other life arenas to even notice or care about such undertaking. Even if you take up martial study, some who lay claim to its knowledge may apportion its wisdom out of sync with your own learning rhythm, in quantities either too large or too small for you to sustain interest, or with an ideology opposite to your ideals. It may be too expensive, require too much exertion or even forbidden if you live in an oppressive community or country. You may strongly believe that martial arts is equated with violence and therefore see it as part of a problem rather than its cure. Or you might feel that martial study is simply not part of your karma. The list of reasons, rationalizations, and barriers is lengthy.

For those who deny that they have a warrior nature or, in all good consciousness, would never activate it, consider this sobering question; What would you do if you saw someone you deeply loved being brutally beaten and you were the only one around to help? It's rare for anyone's warrior instincts not to arouse to such imagined horror. Consider also the peculiar irony that far more people in the world who are not martial artists are called to protect themselves from violence than formal students of the Martial Ways.

Great insight is available for understanding the nature of an assailant, a competitor, or even an obstructing life event by entering a spiritual-based martial dojo. Such a dojo invites one to resolve or, at least, favorably rearrange the puzzles of his or her life. I've seen the dojo turn the ninety-eight pound, sand-faced weakling into a ninety-eight pound powerhouse. I've also seen it convert the brutish into the gentlemanly, the arrogant and aggressive into the compassionate, and the smart into the wise. Wisdom is buried within each of us, perhaps, some deeper than others, but an astute sensei can excavate these complex energies and enable students to build their future success. It doesn't matter where you start your journey. For as the great Vedic scriptures teach, 'As on the inside, so on the outside. As above, so below.' Students of the external arts begin their liberation from the outside, in. Students of the internal arts find their freedom from the inside out. Freedom is freedom, regardless of your starting point.

A radical shift in consciousness is awakening millions of people to their inner potential. It's no coincidence that we are witnessing the emergence and greater acceptance of sacred traditions and alternative modalities of healing as we concurrently discover the mind's uncanny parallel frontier to the extraordinary galaxies swirling about us. All the world's wisdom teachers emphasize that our mind has moment-to-moment accessibility to vast power. Internal martial study opens a direct inroad into this expansive perspective. However, to better understand the nature of Soft technique it is imperative that we investigate and contrast to it the nature of our Hard technique.

When my wife was in high school she told her father that she wanted to become a Special Education teacher. Her father advised her to become a Regular Ed. teacher first, in order for her to better grasp the needs of the Special Ed. student. In that vein, let's begin with a simple overview of the common stages of evolution that martial artists often undergo in their training. I'll begin with obvious Hard skill training and advance into the Soft skills that lay dormant for many. By this process I hope that you will appreciate the vast, intricate and implicate interior powers of the self and those venerable martial paths designed to unlock them.

Why We Train

Essentially, we train in the martial arts to get 'somewhere else.' That is, we initially train to upgrade our current status, or to put it in an internal context, to change the status of our current. Training is always about upgrading; better organization, better energy flow, better muscle tone, better skill sets, etc. Since that 'somewhere' can vary quite widely amongst students, let's review the destinations available and differentiate the internal paths from the external ones. It's helpful to establish some common ground when talking about concepts that might be foreign to a novice or externally oriented student of the martial ways. Occasionally, an idea, principle or technique, thought to be fully grasped during one stage of training, is later found to be faulty, misleading or misinterpreted at higher stages. I once watched an intelligent, adult novice, named Steve, repeatedly fail to execute a three-quarter rotation with his body called for in a basic drill. He was a bright and accomplished chemist for a large pharmaceutical company. When I asked him to explain what he was trying to do I realized that he was doomed to fail because he had this odd notion that the martial arts somehow

transcended the Laws of Physics. He would loose his balance on every attempt. Steve had the erroneous idea that karate was somehow free from the Laws of Physics. Any mystical nature that is attributed to martial arts often comes from applying universal laws in ways that people are simply not accustomed to experiencing.

Destinations Achievable Thru Martial Practice

The Chi Kung master, Dr. Yang Jwing Ming, has outlined five reasons people study any martial art. Casting each reason as a journey would give us the following:

The journey to gain practical, self-protective or competitive skills.

The journey to gain academic (historical, social, cultural) knowledge of the Martial Ways.

The journey to gain greater health and vitality.

The journey for longevity (immortality was a specialized study of the Chinese Taoists).

The journey for character and confidence-building skills, spiritual growth, self-realization, or personal evolution.

Each path above requires a specific focus and a different set of tools and practices, but they are not mutually exclusive treks. We have the capacity to multi-quest several destinations at the same time. However, our ultimate success on any of these paths lies in finding both a reliable vehicle and a competent guide.

It's also important to note that, regardless of the system or style practiced, all sound martial teachings will *expand your awareness* about the subject matter and *increase your skills* and sensitivities within that knowledge field.

We can further subdivide the awareness and the skills into two broad categories; 'Hard' awareness and skills: a sense of the body's biomechanical principles and actions, and 'Soft' awareness and skills: a sense of subtle mind/body energy principles. A well-rounded martial training program will present and balance both of these dimensions.

Vehicles Available To Make The Journey

Some researchers estimate that there are over 4,500 martial arts styles and/or systems existing today, 2,500 in China alone. They range from broad international, multi-thousand member organizations to single family styles, hailing from every corner of the world. All are available transports into and thru the martial experience. The Japanese call their vehicles *ryu*. The Chinese call them *lau*. Each 'School of Teaching' comes with its own stable of sensei, shifu, coaches, or professors. We can purchase our guides live (the sole and primary means of Old World style learning) or take on their teachings indirectly in books or other media. Naturally, some guides are better equipped than others, but you are not going to be able to discern this until you have developed some hands-on knowledge of what different martial vehicles are capable of accomplishing. To put it another way, watching a movie about cars isn't the same as driving them. But driving any car will help you to understand the fundamental nature of car*ness*. The same analogy applies to fighting systems. After you take one for a spin, then, and only then, can you begin to set up a reliable basis for comparison.

My initial vehicle was Okinawan karate. I took minor but intense rides in *Tai Chi Chuan*, *Aikido* and *Kobudo* (weapons) arts. All the martial arts of the world share the same underlying biomechanical principles. However, the manner in which they apply these principles reveals their technical diversity. Later, I discovered that a two-sided or dual nature existed within the older Asian fighting systems. So I souped up to Karate-*Do* to take advantage of my art's missing link. For the traditional arts give us both an obvious, exoteric side and a not so obvious, esoteric nature. As stated earlier, we label this dual nature broadly as the Hard and the Soft side of the Martial Ways. Hard refers to an arts external principles and Soft to its inner ones.

The Conceptual Framework Of Internal And External Martial Arts

In marital arts we use the term internal/soft and external/hard primarily as an academic exercise. It is an attempt to describe a very complex, multi-layered mind/body dynamic. For example, we casually talk about the mind and body as if they were two separate but neighboring entities. However, if we were to take a scalpel and attempt to separate the mind from the body we would find that they are so tightly entwined that there is no blade fine enough to sever them.

This inseparability also exists between the concepts of internal and external martial arts. They are interrelated 'events.' However, in describing the more extreme characteristics of martial practices we can glimpse aspects tending toward one side of the martial paradigm (the external) over another (the internal). Why intellectualize this way? For one, such knowledge and awareness is helpful for nudging students out of training fixations, that is, for preventing them from training in a too limited way. Offering students different ways to express their art encourages them to discover new tools.

Another issue should be addressed. Sometimes we hear mention of internal *versus* external martial art, suggesting that a friction exists between them, as if these two terms represented enemy camps. If you are studying one, you must be denigrating the other. Internal and External concepts are not oppositional modalities of study even though some individuals or martial communities might choose to present them as such. Internal practice is not better than external practice or vice versa. It's best to look at these two descriptors as developmental possibilities. That is, I could take *this* road or *that* road, to reach my destination. It doesn't matter which route you trek. It only matters that you follow your attractions and make some progress. The Great American Architect Frank Lloyd Wright stated that, "Form must fit the function." What you need your martial art for best determines how and what you will take from it.

In truth, it is difficult for most people to step outside of some fundamental and natural biases. Bias is an innate characteristic of human nature. For example, a poet will look at a nude with a literary eye; a surgeon, with the anatomist's eye; a lover, with a sensual inclination; a warrior with a combatant's eye—all valid, but *partial* observations. In similar fashion, most of us will gaze at our arts and/or our opponents from a primary psychological platform, whether we have chosen this perspective consciously or not. Consider, that any choice we make is drawn from a vast set of possibilities. For those of a more mental disposition, parsing perceptions into an internal or external format can be beneficial for stimulating the intellect to activate latent physical powers. Also, to become a truly dynamic teacher, one must affirm and detail the path of experience if he is to activate this path in his disciples.

My martial bias in this book is glaringly obvious. I am completely unashamed about it. My mind was initially cramped toward the mainstream. I looked outward—itself a typical Western bias of an Eastern practice. And I did so for over twenty years of training. I never thought of taking the alternate route of looking *inward*. When I did, I wanted everyone to crane their necks to the marvel that I saw.

At what point does an external movement cross over into the internal lane or vice versa? This book offers a template for viewing these two exciting and interrelated dimensions of practice so that you can answer this question for yourselves.

Internal Martial Ways Practice

The word 'Internal' when applied to the martial arts implies the interior workings of the body/

mind complex. This complex contains a diverse physical, emotional, hormonal, and mental terrain with each facet possessing its own action tendency. The action tendencies of the mind include; thought, intention, will, desire, memory, imagination, intuition, and logic. The action tendencies of the body include neuronal, chemical, electrical, magnetic, glandular/hormonal, aural, photonic, and muscular motions. Internal can also mean hidden from view or hidden from mainstream or conventional thinking. From the Asian perspective, 'internal' generally means the direct and conscious activation and manipulation of an intrinsic life force, an invisible vitalizing energy, the Asians call Qi. To activate our Qi first requires that we relax. Western science has been formulating a hypothesis about such a force as a confluence of many subtle energies working in synergy with one another. The New Practical Chinese English Dictionary lists eight basic definitions for Qi with an additional ninety-three definitions by various combinations. The eight are: Air, gas, vapor, atmosphere; Breath; Spirit character; Influence; Bearing, manner; Smell, odor; To be angry, or indignant; To provoke, to goad.

Because Qi has multiple definitions, both banal and sublime, it is easy to see how a Westerner could miss its value in one's training, because the term, unfamiliar to most, also encompasses a wide variety of phenomenon, not all martial. In and of itself, the very notion of an invisible force seems illusive to most Westerners. However, the use of Qi in the martial arts has been embraced for centuries. 1st century Chinese are recorded practicing therapeutic movements utilizing gymnastic movements coupled with specific breathing patterns called *Daoyin* that would later be merged with Shaolin Chuan Fa techniques adding hidden leverage to oust assailants, to outscore competitors or, if extended into the spiritual realm, as practiced in monastic life, to overcome interior resistances and merge with the Infinite. We acknowledge this latter undertaking as the enlightenment process.

Karate is a class of Asian fighting arts indigenous to the Japanese Ryukyu Islands and mainland Japan. Karate systems called *ryu* (literally, meandering river) flowed into and saturated mainland Japanese curiosity in the early 1900's and then flooded the rest of the world. Martial historians postulate that Okinawan karate impacted the development of both modern Japanese styles and Korean Tae kwon Do. An important artifact in today's Asian fighting systems, particularly those that evolved from pre-industrial traditions, are the layered and complex kinesthetic treatises called *kata*. Performed either solo or as partnered forms, these kata preserve old world, time-tested, civil-protection

techniques on one level, while teaching its practitioners how to manage subtle energy currents on another. Mainstream American culture initially embraced Karate for its topical self-defense practicalities and as a competitive physical discipline that could transform the body into a great tool of precision and power. Prolonged practice even had the effect of sharpening one's perceptions and expanding awareness. But most of us caught up in the rapid expansion of the arts in the 1960's and 1970's missed kata's internal codice as an *art within an art* where we could tap into other powerful synchronistic forces.

Karatedo/Kempo - I will use *Karatedo* and *Kempo* as terms to imply both a physical and spiritual teaching. Chinese martial arts of Buddhist influence were referred to as *Quan* or *Chuan Fa*, literally interpreted as the Clasped Hand Dharma. The fist clutches the Buddha's teachings. The Japanese called these Chuan Fa arts *Kempo*. Later, the Okinawans placed their Chinese-influenced arts under the general label, Karate, a mix of Chinese martial influence with their indigenous island fighting techniques—and when the spiritual element was present—karatedo. Karate's history owes a great deal to the influences of its ancestral arts. But Chinese monastic tradition themselves based their fighting arts upon even older, Indian Buddhist *Vajramukti* teachings of non-violent self-defense, healing, health-nourishing, and spiritual discipline. The quest of the temple monastic was to transcend conflict altogether by using the martial arts as a ladder of ritual practices and experiences to this end. Whenever you come across the terms, *karate, karatedo,* or *kempo* you must keep in mind that their modern context often deviates greatly from their ancestral one. Many of today's martial arts proponents no longer ally themselves to any formal spiritual practices.

Do (Chinese, *Tao*) is an Asian philosophical concept that emerged from deep introspection and generations-long ascetic practices and inquiries. The concept of the *Do* or *Way* dates back into China's mythical antiquity. The Japanese term *Do* and its Chinese predecessor, *Tao*, describes a Way of Being. This *Way of Being* is cultivated through spiritual or ritual practice—meditation being one of its primary methods. Ritual practice aims at aligning oneself with the naturally flowing action of our universe. Professor Malcolm David Eckle of Boston University believes that ritual practice forms a "mezzocosm," a middle path or bridge, linking one's inside (micro) and outside (macro) worlds. The Do also defines a way of life influenced by disciplined self-study, one valuing spiritual existence alongside and in balance with material existence. At its core, the Do of martial arts aims to dissolve conflict absolutely in the same way that the external martial artist seeks to vanquish a physical enemy.

Internal Martial Ways, in its most encompassing definition, is the art of consciously activating, refining, and expressing subtle or fine layers of martial technique. These subtle dimensions include psychological, emotional, bio-energetic or Soft/Qi principles within a spiritual context of existence as part of karate's power matrix. Old world Okinawan karate masters referred to the most tangible see and touch nature of karate's internal principles as *kiko* (spirit/breath), and *chinkutsu* or *chin-quchi* (sinew/bone/energy control). These terms were used to describe often-concealed aspects of heightened physical, and sometimes metaphysical, energy management practices and principles. I must restate here that there are advanced martial practitioners who do not attribute extra-ordinary powers to anything but a heightened body alignment/sensitivity or attunement. We will consider their perspective in chapter Five in the section entitled, 'Trick Or Chi'.

External Martial Ways Practice

External karate is the expression of the physical, overt, hard-wired or obvious gross nature of martial technique and principles. Where the Internal systems deal mostly with Qi management, External karate deals with what the Chinese term, '*Li*' or strength, as applied through gross muscular tension. We can refer to this basic tension model as the art's biomechanical nature, or in dojo vernacular, as its Hard features. External karate deals primarily with the actions of the musculoskeletal and nervous systems as they directly relate to and enhance the combative properties of speed, power, strength, endurance, balance, reactivity and flexibility in a Cartesian/Newtonian context. By this philosophical/scientific context I mean that our minds easily register and accept bodily actions that conform to the most obvious and commonly held direct expressions of the laws of physics regarding the use of physical power, through shifting weight and balance in the extension and retraction of the limbs. However, we rarely extend these same laws into alternate dimensions of movement. In a general sense, external karate training tends to place little or far less conscious emphasis upon refining the body's covert energy and communication systems. This is mostly due to the fact that the main populace doesn't know what they are. These subtle energy currents and inner events fall outside of the simplistic, conventional, linear cause and effect, kick/punch model where 'hard' is all

you need. As you will see, external karate relies more on a fixed, and sometimes rigid, understanding of the laws of physics. I call this state a Common Mind, primitive, or gut ideology. For example, most people would readily agree that a well-developed muscular person should naturally possess more power than a thin or seemingly underdeveloped physique. Yet, when it comes to demonstrations of internal power this is not always the case. It becomes more an issue of inner organization than of outward shape or appearance. Certainly, internal power can and is greatly aided by a healthy and toned physique.

By contrast, when properly organized and applied, one's internal forces can amplify gross physical power because they draw from a confluence of emotional, psychological and spiritual wellsprings that are often restricted by our conditioned sense of physical laws. Your punches will possess more thrust, your torso will torque more intensely, your stances will become harder to uproot, your blocks will feel like iron rods and your mind will become unbendable and single-pointed.

Are Internal And External Arts Mutually Exclusive Practices?
No. You need a body to have energy and energy to have a body. To analogize, every coin has three sides: front, back, and rim. The rim, however thin, reveals the inseparability of the coin's two faces. Each side supports, links, and defines the other. This two-sided coinness may have been the preliminary understanding of early Asian philosophers who challenged the interdependent nature of all phenomena. This two-faces-on-one-coin concept led some Asian philosophers to seek a way to walk the rim of the two competing polarities of human nature such as good versus evil, for example. The kempo masters observed that all human actions posses a dual nature. Upon their reflections regarding the nature of self, they asked if it was possible to step off the 'Wheel of Suffering' (*Samsara*) brought on by the dualistic thinking. For to flip one side 'up' was simultaneously to flip the other side 'down.' Good could oppose bad or good could complement bad depending upon one's perspective. Exclusively focusing on one coin side would conceal the other from the mind's eye (because this action was by one's own choosing, it was considered a form of ignorance by Buddhists). The coins hidden other side still existed, just not in the mind of the one-sided thinker. This three-sided coin analogy is also a truism regarding the underlying nature of martial technique. It is impossible to draw a precise line dividing Hard from Soft style technique. This has confused many regarding the nature of internal martial arts study.

As mentioned earlier, some masters don't see the need to discuss a term like Qi because, under the right circumstances, when the body is working harmoniously, power just flows. I agree. Power flows when the proper physical and mental 'architecture,' or overall structure, is achieved. In my teaching opinion however, defining and categorizing various physical and mental organizations into layered types of techniques equips the intelligent student with a more fluid and conscious level of tactical execution, especially when diverse skill sets must be summoned into play.

Until the last quarter of the 19th century American karate-ka *en masse* expressed little interest in or awareness of flipping their martial coin from its external benefits to its internal ones. Mainstream Americans initially perceived the art of karate solely for its effective but superficial benefits. When Americans first embraced the practical, self-protective aspects of karate, they doubted much else existed beyond the surface of a strong kick or punch. This bias obscured internal training values by burying them under more topical ones. We did not embrace the spiritual implications or the refined internal infrastructure inherent in the Asian fighting arts because we just couldn't see it. It would take over thirty years for this awakening to occur in the United States with the maturing of its home-grown teachers.

The Difference Between 'Karate' and 'Karatedo'

The label 'karate' or 'karatedo' as a retail register may not imply the actual teachings of a dojo. The term 'Do,' as stated earlier, refers to an art's spiritual essence. Some karate-labeled schools teach 'Do' principles. Some karatedo-labeled schools do not. Many karatedo schools blend homegrown, informal spiritual teachings into their teachings or embrace and intertwine formal disciplines like Zen, Buddhism, Shinto, Taoism, Christianity, or Muslim philosophies into their training. Here mundane martial practices are interwoven with spiritual ones through the addition of meditation, prayer and ritual. When we say 'spiritual' practice we are distinguishing an attitudinal platform of training. An atmosphere of cooperation and compassion exists in a spiritually grounded dojo rather than hostile competition and insensitivity. Occasionally, we also find a level of individual initiative and intuitive orientation that, for reasons unknown, align some students in the seemingly most superficial of circumstances or environments to activate highly elevated spiritual principles. But this is not commonplace. The primary difference between Hard and Soft martial teachings is that the 'Do' or 'soft' side creates an awareness of a much larger scope of interaction extending beyond a single

material goal or egocentric viewpoint. For a better understanding of the personal nature of spiritual pursuit and understanding in the martial arts I recommend you read the *Soul Polisher's Apprentice, A Martial Kumite about Personal Evolution* (Wind School, 2007)

What Internal Practice Offers That External Training Does Not

Internal Karatedo practice, combined with sound external principles, offers the full face of Martial Ways study consistent with the central philosophies of the Asian spiritual lineage masters. Karate's external nature yields many positive qualities that are more than adequate for sustaining a life-long interest in one's art. Externally sound, reality-based, karate systems provide effective civil protection, exhibition and/or competition skills. The issue is not that one studies either an internal or external martial art, or that one preference or emphasis on training is better than another. Such statements can only be made in regards to the personal relevancy of one's training regime. It may be more relevant that a student initially study the Hard aspects of his art, while another explores its Soft nuances. Often it is merely by coincidence that a beginning student finds him or herself in a school emphasizing one trait over another. It is natural and understood by professional teachers that novice students cannot distinguish any categorizations of technique without first immersing themselves in their discipline. According to one American karate master, the true adept is one who marries the Hard and Soft elements of their art. Of course, this becomes problematic when one cannot distinguish Hard from Soft values, lacks awareness of the complementary nature of these types of skills, or is blocked either by inside or outside forces from realizing their existence or relevancy.

Those Who Deny Hidden Or Secret Dimensions To Martial Ways Training

It is normal for people working with internal energy to draw skepticism from those who are unfamiliar with it, who do not believe in Qi or its value by reducing its effects to mere tricks of suggestion or deception, or who are awaiting the hard science to prove its existence. But the issue of whether there are hidden or no hidden techniques, visible or invisible forces in martial arts, is mostly semantic, unless you are referring to the deliberate withholding of information from someone seeking it. Whether you chose to call a yet-to-be-revealed teaching or unperceived energy a secret, is moot. For example, in 2000 I published a large article in a trade journal in which I briefly explained the bioelectric principles of a certain type of blocking action. No one ever wrote or asked me about this technique though I am sure few readers were aware of it prior. There are treasures literally buried right under the noses (blocking actions and fist positions) of martial artists who have never approached their techniques in this manner.

The important point is that professional teachers clearly see that broad fields of martial knowledge and artful body maneuvering are unfamiliar to most of their beginning students. By 'broad informational fields' I am referring to principles rather than to any individual technique. Individual technique is always the physical expression of a movement principle such as moving from the center, timing, body organization, etc. A novice does not understand the fine mechanics or whole body synergy behind basic actions like punches/blocks/kicks/locks, and he or she will lack effective combative strategies as a result. A novice knows little about the value of the traditional patterns called kata, or the effects of Qi, (subtle breath and mental intention) upon his physical actions, no less how to control them. But all enduring and sensitive students *will* enter these knowledge fields over time.

Though internal training has the ability to generate extraordinary power, I will first address some core theoretical and philosophical considerations while saving a glimpse into the practical side for the final portion of this book.

It is my hope that readers will come to discover the benefits of internal manipulation. This book is a challenge to lift the mainstream martial perspective to new heights of self-expression. In my experience, the older martial generation generously laid down a solid foundation for the West to study but, for whatever reason, we mostly overlooked the martial art's more nuanced lessons. Perhaps, the Asian masters realized that part of the West's edification was to first sharpen our over-hungry, round eyes to see beyond the art's surface realities. There is no blame for what could have been taught in the past any more than casting blame for what American martial artists overlooked of karate's depth with its welcomed inception in the United States. This book simply hopes to illuminate some powerful martial concepts that may be unknown to many practitioners.

Why Many Martial Artists Do Not See Their Arts Internal Components

My earliest guides in Okinawan karate only transmitted to me karate's outer nature. For reasons, intentional or otherwise, they omitted its interior proportions. And I failed to realize the existence of these hidden components for the next twenty-five years of practice! Thus is the power of the mind to fix our perceptions so strongly. I was simply content to punch and kick my way through life in a

basic, this is what I was told to do, kind of way. Then one day a mysterious technical event jostled my brain. At that instant, I knew, with great certainty, that I had missed a critical, key feature of my art. A simple wristlock escape that I had practiced thousands of times previously, suddenly yielded an outcome entirely disproportionate to my effort going into it. My seasoned partner caught the anomaly as well. We had not been trained to see a concealed principle working through our postures that had distributed a much greater current of energy than we had previously observed. My action was unusually powerful. We properly called the phenomenon a *Qi-reaction*. Over the next decade and a half we began to unravel its mystery.

We posed several critical questions with no idea that they would forever alter our training paradigm. Was it possible that some, if not all, of the Okinawan and Japanese 'Hard style' martial arts, had this soft, internal power infrastructure embedded into their kata? Was it possible that kata, in addition to its topical self-defense value, was actually the legacy designed to convey this other information forward? We knew that our art shared similar techniques to Naha and Shuri-Te based Okinawan martial lineages and certainly their ancestor arts in China. What better way to transmit this knowledge than through this mystic warrior dance. For it was rapidly becoming evident to us that kata was not just an expedient formulaic biomechanical response to physical threat, as the US kata orthodoxy has maintained since the 1950's but also a time capsule of highly refined, subtle energy actions—even metaphysical principles. The deeper we pressed our hypothesis, the more stability we found in the arrangement of some traditional forms. The observation exhilarated me like a young boy discovering a dinosaur bone in his backyard. I craved to find the whole creature—and if possible, to bring it back to life. The hunt was on.

While pursuing our theory I also came to appreciate the opposing rationale, that proper body alignment was the only standing 'mystery' behind extraordinary physical endeavor.

I had initial difficulty with those teachers who believed that my personal experiences were just the result of better body dynamics. How could *they* fail to see this extraordinary realm? I soon came to realize my own naiveté. I only saw, with my obvious bias, their failure to address those covert mental and physical dimensions of training. I had narrowly aligned with the majority of martial artists who had had the inner perspective excluded from their curriculum. Certainly mine was not the only valued experience martial artists were having.

My art's soft underbelly had only dominated my senses due to its complete absence from my early training focus. The missing facet only appeared to be separate from bone and muscle organization, when in truth it was always inseparably linked to it. I had been the blind one. I was the one with limited understanding. The truth had been sitting patiently in front of me the whole time.

I could analogize that our peculiar views are akin to a focal point on a visual foreground or background. Although we might fail to take in the detail of background images when fixing our gaze on the foreground ones, the background objects don't cease to exist. So, if you suddenly saw the background detail of your art, after years of neglect, you might take up a crusade to point out this missing component to others as visually impaired as yourself.

A myopic perception pervades our martial arts today. The result has caused a spiritual defoliation of broad sectors of the mainstream martial community. There is no one to blame. Many teachers fail to point to the background of their arts because no one pointed out its value to them. This book takes up the crusade to bring the technique behind the technique into focus.

The value or merit we attach to our arts depicts both our level of awareness and personal relevancy. It's not uncommon, for example, to meet people who carry strong biases toward martial styles outside of their own disciplines to the point of denigrating them or even physically challenging the proponents of other viewpoints. The real issue isn't how my art stacks up to your art in the ring since few men actually express the ideals of their systems. What's important is recognizing the degree of synergy between Soft and Hard techniques underlying all the martial arts, even if only felt by the student or unspoken by the teacher. For where do you draw the line between proper body alignment and mental involvement, respiratory integration and/or energy (Qi) infusion?

The 'proper body mechanic' model serves most. However, by analogy, where does foreground end and background begin? Isn't such a division initially a degree of optical attraction? I feel this analogy makes an elemental observation about the nature of our everyday working mind, what Buddhists call 'ordinary' or 'surface mind'. We tend to look first and foremost at what is familiar to us (in many cases this means, what we have been conditioned to see). That is, we look at what is near or dear at hand, or what catches our eye (or told is near or dear, if we are a student), until we learn to look independently or elsewhere. So all of us stand somewhere on Mt. Meru, that great metaphorical Buddhist mountain representing reality, occasionally catching a blur of significant, but unrecognizable, images on the far horizon and perhaps, if lucky enough, we may discover our own authentic power.

INTERNAL KARATE

Consider that scientists once viewed an atom as a single tiny unit. Broad swaths of a once skeptical world scientific community, after hot debate, came to agree with this reality, which was later decisively proven. It was the best scientists could see of the minuteness of the physical world given existing technology and mindsets. With further advances, scientists saw even smaller particles- protons and neutrons bound by a strong force around which electrons whizzed. This newer vision took precedent. Today, Quantum physicists see even smaller particles called quarks, muons and gluons and hypothesize that even tinier strings of energy exist inside these quarks. The persons who first saw the quarks jarred the sensitivities of those who only saw single atoms. Who was right? Who was wrong? No one. We simply evolve one foothold at a time. As we lift ourselves to other vantages, the nature of reality takes on an ever-vibrant new shape. This same process plays itself out in each and every individual's thinking life so that what comes into view is unique to your vantage point. Just as there are many people today who do not have any awareness about the existence of the atom, no less tiny hypothetical strings of energy composing it, there are those who have no idea how far martial culture has advanced their knowledge of martial technique.

PART TWO
MIND MATTERS

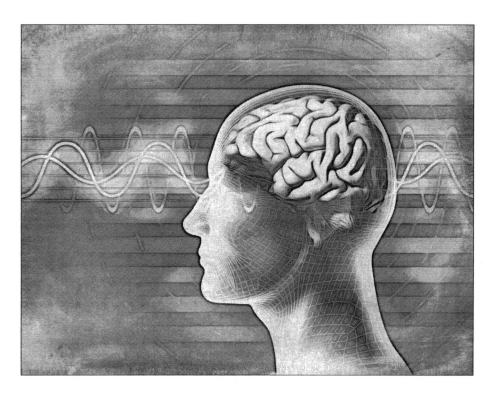

"Old Beliefs that need to go;
That the brain creates consciousness. In reality, it's the other way around."
Deepak Chopra, Rudolph Tanzai, Super Brainl

"All that we are is the result of what we have thought."
Buddha

Mind Matters

However you describe your martial persona; as neophyte, intermediate or seasoned practitioner, *uchi deshi* (live-in disciple), sensei, tournament performer, competitor, action movie star, or arm chair hobbyist—we are not all 'moving' with the same mind behind our actions. Our outsides may look remarkably similar but our insides stand worlds apart. Beneath our skins lay a broad range of mentalities, of comprehensions, of degrees of instinct, emotion, intellect, intuition, self-awareness and destinies. Even the most banal daily activity reveals diverse mental platforms motivating them. The often ambiguous or abstract arena of 'the mind' is where the finer distinctions of masterful versus mediocre martial technique exist. This is true regardless of the discipline - from *Aikido* to *Zui Quan* (Drunken Boxing). The internal masters long ago discovered that the wisdom of the martial arts was to be found in plumbing the depth of the mind.

The inner seekers adopted the Martial Ways as a physical means of penetrating the workings of the non-physical world for clues to the power, meaning, and balance of life. Meditative movement let them peer into their bodies to witness their mental patterns and Subtle Energy Body at work. Their adoption of a physical discipline as an instrument for mental and spiritual study paralleled the search of the Indian warrior caste, the *Kshatriya*, and the Yogis who sought to vanquish external or internal obstacles, expand their reality, and come to terms with their own mortality. Spiritually-grounded martial arts not only prevent our divides from widening, they offer clear solutions to fill them. Well-rounded martial arts systems today engender true and lasting confidence, restore physical and mental balance, and present a wide range of tools for resolving both physical and non-physical conflicts.

The monastic martial disciple joined in the quintessential campaign to face his authentic nature and bridge those precipitous gulfs that separated him from the source of his being.

However, while our tangible techniques and practices have been well documented, many schools still remain grossly inarticulate, even mute, about the role the mental faculties play in the success of physical technique. Perhaps, it is because our mind seems so close to us that it appears invisible, abstract, or a passive, taken-for-granted passenger. This however, is not true. Just as we can sharpen, refine, or temper our physical techniques, we can also heighten our mental ones. If the mind and body are intimately related, than honing our perceptions must add to our physical prowess.

Let's now explore some important psychological and philosophical characteristics of the mind to better understand the soil out of which primary internal concepts have emerged.

THE THREE PHILOSOPHICAL TERRAINS OF KARATEDO PRACTICE

Integrate

Stabilize

Attune

THE PHYSICAL NATURE OF KARATEDO
'A philosophy of Integrity'

A couple cannot give birth without a sperm and an egg no matter how lustful their desire to procreate. The academic cannot birth ideas without activating his three pounds of electrified grey matter sparking in its bony chalice. The carpenter cannot craft a custom cabinet without deft hands to push his table saw and keen eyesight to guide it. The opera singer needs vocal chords to carry her aria to the audience. The jujitsu adept can't pin his opponent without limbs and a torso to create a center of gravity. Bodiless, none of us have a vehicle for our willing to accomplish anything in the world of matter.

The hard world takes on meaning and value precisely because we have the ability to interact with matter. Our facile physical forms leverage, hurl, punch, grasp, assemble, dismantle, release, charge, discharge, retreat, open, close, fill, empty, etc., within a precise time and space to both maintain and to advance our material positions.

Our body is the ever-faithful servant of our mind. Body is ready to sacrifice for our every wish and whim. Continual practice in the physical dimension of martial arts reveals and promotes a philosophy of efficiency and integration between what we want from the material world and how our physical form can best acquire it.

PART 2

PSYCHIC & EMOTIONAL NATURE OF KARATEDO
'A Philosophy of Stability'

Our mind and emotions represent our psychic, neuronal, hormonal and chemical interface between our inner and outer worlds. Karatedo's meditative training (found in its ritual solo practices) gives us a window into our own streaming natures and brings us face to face with our precious, internal cargo. In karatedo we learn to empty out our impurities, imbalances, angers, hesitations, stiffness or clumsiness, and fill instead with strength, courage, resolve, stamina and grounding. Emptying and filling is the way of Karatedo life. Emptying and filling is the way of all life.

According to professor Robert C. Solomon at the University of Texas our emotions provide us with the internal tactics for dealing with hostilities. We don't just *have* emotional responses, like fear or anger, we *do* fear and we *do* anger until a resolution occurs. *Doing* fear enables us to respond to or avoid dangerous situations. Summoning anger asserts our boundaries to repel uninvited intruders. These active E-motions (energies-in-motion) regulate our interior world.

To engage our world fully we must awaken and enlist our psychic and emotional energies. The physical body can't do it alone. A primary function of our mental and emotional faculties is to maintain interior equilibrium. Study of this aspect of martial arts reveals and promotes a philosophy of stability.

THE SPIRITUAL NATURE OF KARATEDO:
'A Philosophy of Attunement'

A pebble dropped into the pond affects the entire pond and its surrounding environment, not just at the point of impact on the water's surface. The pebble's descent fans the air and roils the water. It vibrates the sandy pond bottom. Its ripples never cease, even though our senses can no longer detect them. Likewise, a change in any single dimension of self (mental, emotional, physical) instantly affects the others.

When the ripples of the pebble and of our own actions pass beyond our ability to detect them they enter into an infinitesimally small, yet powerful, field that physicists call the Quantum universe. This universe is the energetic loam of life. Its energy fields engulf us just as our human energies embrace them.

All our actions whether begun as mental, physical, or spiritual events ripple indefinitely throughout time and space and, like the falling pebble, cause tiny but significant changes at the vibrational level of existence.

The Doka, (Way student) learns to accept the world as more than meets the eye. Spiritual practice reveals and promotes a philosophy of attunement to this vast vibratory sea. Attunement is the act of brining oneself into harmony with the vitality of the universe. Even quelling violence with violence is an attempt, extreme or superficial, to bring the world into some measure of peaceful coexistence. Spiritually, our adversaries represent fragments of our outer world attempting to unify with our inner world. Only when both the outer and inner rebellion is quelled can we claim true spiritual mastery over our arts.

4 PRINCIPLES OF ACTION AND BEHAVIOR

Principle 1
Seeing is not always believing, but believing is a form of seeing
What you believe shapes what you see. It will shape your behaviors and manifest what you receive from life. This explains why some sensei place biomechanical and/or subtle energy categorizations under a single umbrella of proper alignment or structure, while others see something entirely different. If you focus solely on external objectives then only those outside goals will present their value. Where you stand is what you see (believe). Stand in a different spot to alter your beliefs.

Principle 2
The body/mind is a one-piece unit
Synergy arises from the parts of the body and its primary systems contributing to the whole, and the whole contributing to the parts. Isolating any of the parts from the whole fragments mind and body, reduces the potential of martial technique, and only grants the *illusion* of power.

Principle 3
The human entity is an open-ended and extensive system
We do not end at the limits of our physical form. Our mind, with its force-generating intentions, is part of a greater weave. Our outside environment, consisting of events and things, forms part of our extended body. The universe with its known and unknown galaxies and forces forms part of our extended body. The spiritual masters tell us that even our opponents are part of our extended body. We are, at any given time and by degrees, in constant communication with our many extensions.

Principle 4
The body's biomechanics compliment its bioenergetics
The proper biomechanical structure of one's physical technique generally compliments the energetic or non-physical technique. However, the reverse statement is not necessarily true. Proper energetic technique can be complimented by proper biomechanical technique but it is not always requisite. A physical body correctly aligned with its subtle energies will maximize its physical force.

Personal Journey

My curiosity with 'mind' and 'self' was piqued during my post black belt training. It percolated for years before I actually took a serious, academic look at the relationship between my mental and physical movements. Initially, I gave a great deal more attention to *how* I moved i.e., how I could punch or kick better, before I became interested in *why* I moved. I felt this latter quest might explain some of the deeper impulses behind my actions. I even started wondering why we moved at all. For example, when I say, "I move," who or what exactly is the 'I' referred to? If my mind moves my physical body, what moves my mind? If some outside influence or spirit moves my mind, is it appropriate to ask, "Who or what moves my spirit? In fact, "Who is even asking these questions?" To avoid this chicken or egg dilemma I toned down my inquisition by personalizing my line of reasoning. I asked instead, "How do my mind and body move together?" and "How can my mind and body work better?" As I looked into these questions I observed five primary life movements behind all human interaction:

The Five Underlying Life Movements

If we do not confine 'movement' to a single realm of being, that is, solely as a mental or a physical action, we could distill all human behavior into five primary states or five primary motions. At any given point in time our mind/body is either moving or fixed along the following scale:

1. Soul deadening misery. This is the ultimate stuckness of being. In this state the mind rigidifies. The ego becomes so "me heavy" it cannot budge. One feels empty. Life becomes a black hole of inertia.

> *Sadly, a former student of mine committed the first mass killings in the history of his town. He stabbed to death his mother, brother, and best fried in a psychotic rage. He was caught by the police and sentenced to life imprisonment. He had lost his mind.*

2. Moving into darkness. Our life actions move toward gradual degrees of disintegration, lack of clarity, illusion, isolation, separateness, disease, disorganization or dysfunction. Darkness metaphorically represents negative, life-defeating, vitality-draining qualities. Moving into darkness weights our life. It casts a gloom over our day. We lose more than we gain even though we may suffer from the illusion of advance.

A female student at a neighboring martial arts school admitted that her teachers verbally abused her and others. Yet, she continued to attend the classes. Abusive teachers, parents, and all self-abusers often steal from our natures far more then they return.

3. Holding middle ground (holding to one's current state of being): No living thing is completely still. Our quintessential molecular motions reveal a basic and incessant vacillation. But the majority of people in the world only move over a limited range of territory—on good days rocking forward into health or clarity of mind, but on off days, sliding backwards into over-exertion, fatigue, or mental fogginess. In this tide-like rhythm we do not get any smarter or dumber, faster or slower, richer or poorer. We neither gain nor lose significant ground.

One student, who had achieved the brown belt grade, found himself dealing with an increasingly difficult weight problem. The weight issue affected his back limiting his training and forcing him to temporarily drop formal classes. He would return after many chiropractic adjustments with renewed purpose, only to drop out again for the same reasons. A cycle of rally, set back, rally, set back, stretched on year after year.

4. Moving into the light: By the 'light' is meant that our life force moves us toward higher degrees of integration, health, wholeness, clarity, confidence, and positive, life-enhancing qualities. We advance in a whole or complete manner. Our load lightens. Life brightens. Richer meaning and expansive dimensionality enters our day. More is gained than lost.

An arrogant, but accomplished middle-aged entrepreneur joined the dojo mainly to fight. He hated wearing a white belt and inwardly begrudged performing kata while the senior students engaged in free-style sparring. But over time, after intense dialog and training, he began to see that his fight lust had been motivated by a repressed anger from unwelcome events in his early childhood. He began to shed his edginess and self-conceit, took a real concern for others, and saw his life lighten and improve in every category.

5. Bliss: The sages tell us that the experience of pure joyfulness, serenity within movement, or "arriving home," is ours for the claiming. Bliss reflects our purest contentment with life. Conflicts are transcended. The ego's perpetual flame of self-limitation is extinguished. Feelings of ecstasy, *nirvana*, or god realization flow unimpeded.

> *A thirty five year old Indian man sat under a Bodhi tree after years of sacrifice and self-searching on the nature of reality. His mind suddenly awakened to a path beyond conflict and he was thereafter called the Buddha.*

A completely satisfied human will exist in a state of perfect balance, or what the sages have paradoxically described as 'stillness entering movement/movement entering stillness' There is no need to 'move' in this state because theoretically, all desires are met. Perfect satiety means being filled in every way. But to progress toward such a state requires that we empty our old ways to make room for the new. Authentic karatedo is the *Way of Emptying*. This path gives us the opportunity to pour and refill. Along this 'emptying way' we will confront some important philosophical considerations:

The Universe Only Loans Us Energy

The universe generously and unconditionally invests energy into each and every one of us so that we can meet our destinies. However, human energy, in all its various captured forms, is only on loan to us. We will not have life indefinitely. Some day we must pass our energy along so that other forms of existence can have their go at it. Yet, right now, each of us is distinctively configured to transform our life energy and put it back into circulation with a different and meaningful spin. This marks the special and sacred quality to and value of all human life.

The Enemy Is Not Always Human

Martial Ways introduced by military and village experts help people to combat physical enemies. The early monastic and spiritual masters realized that some of our enemies were not always physical. The enemy could also represent other types of divides or conflicts, such as the social and psychological rifts that exist, for example, between a girlfriend and boyfriend, husband and wife, brother and sister, employee and boss, bully and victim, even between our own imbalances, expectations and reality. These Asian temple pioneers expanded the concept of enemy to include not just hostile persons, but maligned beliefs and ideologies, fears and delusions, emotional disorders, disorganized thinking—essentially any thing or event that opposed or oppressed our core nature, including self-ignorance about the workings of our own mind.

It is not hard to see how we sometimes behave in ways that make us our own worst enemy. The etymology of the word *enemy* derives from Latin *inimicus*, meaning hostile, not a friend. Our enemy

56

is not of us or like us. We see an enemy spinning opposite from us, at odds with our desires. The Asian inner warriors reasoned that if one developed skillful mental attitudes, along with physical skills, they could lessen or eliminate most of life's conflicts, including embedded cycles of negativity that lured hardships to them. Buddhist Kempo masters interwove this upper tier understanding into a conflict-resolution strategy and planted it squarely into their physical practices. At the highest levels of training they sought to extinguish the very concept of the enemy in their own minds.

It's human nature to fear and to desire. These two emotions often walk hand in hand. You might desire to lose weight, yet fear not losing it. You might desire to earn a black belt, yet simultaneously fear the possibility you might fail at getting it. How many youths wish they could defeat their bullies yet, fear the repercussions of getting beaten up by them? We are always moving between degrees of fear and desire. Either way, we must expend effort, however trivial, to claim a desire or confront a fear. To satisfy physical hunger, for example, we must get up, walk to the fridge, make a food selection, prepare the food, and eat it. To defeat the competition we must rouse our body, set our resolve, overcome our concerns of injury or failure, attack and/or defend with precision within specific rules of engagement. Life moves because it yearns to get somewhere. Fear and desire ignite action. But the very act of fearing or desiring simultaneously creates the possibility of pain and suffering if our desires can't be satisfied or our fears cannot be conquered and consume us.

Buddhist masters observe that both extreme desire and extreme fear are root causes of personal suffering. The Buddha and his followers saw quite clearly that it was part of the human condition to suffer when desires met impasses or fear tramples us. With keen observation they saw in kempo practice a means to unmask the true face of conflict as the illusion of an over-grasping mind.

Five Source Ways To Fill Your Divides

We can fill our divides by seeking our personal truth through conscientious, integrative, and explorative practices and rituals. The Greek philosopher Socrates was right, "Know thyself," and by implication, the Asian kempo masters followed with, "Act accordingly!" The idea is to find a path, find an attitude, find a 'Way,' a 'Do,' that challenges us to fulfill our legacy. We can all benefit from tools that free us from all manner of bindings that hold us back from realizing our clearest goals, dreams, and potential.

INTERNAL KARATE

There are five source pursuits, five fundamental entry points outlined below, embedded in a wide range of world disciplines, including the martial arts, that are available for filling our personal and/ or professional gaps or divides, extracting our core truths, and linking us back to our Source powers. No one path is intrinsically better than another. Each carries its own appeal. These Source methods are not mutually exclusive. You can pursue several courses at once, but if you are limited by time you should choose one or two as your dominant tools to avoid spreading your focus too thin.

The Five Fundamental Practices
1. **Intellectual pursuits/practices:** using your mind to investigate the nature of mind/self/reality to fill your desires/divide(s)
2. **Devotional pursuits/practices:** expanding your heart through love and compassion to embrace life fully to fill your desires/divides
3. **Karmic pursuits/practices:** studying the cause and effect of mental and physical actions to fill your desires/divides
4. **Health pursuits/practices:** using vitality practices to transcend or fill your desires/divides
5. **Mantric pursuits/practices:** A mantra is a sacred word or chant. Mantric pursuits use vibrational practices (rhythmic, audible, or silent chanting) to transcend or fill your desires/divides.

A senior Buddhist kempo master once remarked to me that the martial arts, in a broad sense, could be likened to a karmic or health yoga. With just a little effort his position was not hard to see. For the practice of Karatedo, as a spiritual discipline, is really an underlying study of human conflict. The goal is to reduce our frictions, whether the actions are directed toward preventing a bully from ruffling us or toward reducing anxiety about our careers, relationships or mortality. These arts bring fresh observations and intuitions through ritual practices to extrapolate ultimate truths about our behaviors.

The kempo masters steeped themselves in philosophical study and discourse. They saw martial discipline as a microcosm of life. Its multi-dimensional practices revealed the nature of man-to-man conflicts and offered remedies to quell personal oppositions. One Indian master, Nargajuna (c. 150-250 CE) in particular, left us his penetrating tactical philosophy:

TACTICAL PHILOSOPHY

"Believe nothing,
no matter where you read it, or who said it,
no matter if I have said it,
unless it agrees with your own reason
and your own common sense."

Buddha

The Mind Conjures—The Body Obeys

Every man, woman and child by their behaviors, whether conscious or not, acts out a living philosophy. Decisions, repeatedly performed, represent the tactics of our beliefs. True students of the Martial Way are well versed in tactics. Tactics are the specific actions by which we accomplish any goal. We may choose driving over bicycling to get to the store, execute a kick over a grappling maneuver to defeat a competitor, or act out a compassionate behavior over an aggressive one to get our wishes met. The Chinese esoteric masters studied tactics in intricate detail. According to the work

of the late Kempo scholar, Nagaboshi Tomio, the 2nd Century Indian Master Nagarjuna provided us with a tactical theory for the Kempo *kumite* (exchange). We can apply Nagarjuna's philosophical logic and teachings both to our daily problems as well as to dangerous physical situations. At a very basic external level, related to life and death processes, Nagarjuna observed four main responses to any attacking enemy.

We kill the enemy

We are killed by the enemy

We evade the enemy

We transform the enemy

Each successive response 'slays' the previous, changing the situation in some way. These four possibilities form the basis of all knowledge within esoteric kempo teachings as they pass through the Buddhist's Three Gates of Experience: Mind, Body and Speech.

Nagarjuna's Tactical Philosophy offers us a critical perspective for assessing and implementing impending action. He reveals how the mind distills and determines our physical reactions. Although Nagarjuna's original perspective applied the four responses to warfare we can also apply them as a tactical guideline toward any problem, any conflict, inside or outside of the dojo, including healthy competition where we strive for personal excellence. These tactics can also be applied, in Nagaboshi's words, "to the battle of one's spirit within a clouded consciousness." Broadening the four responses to include any conflicted arena of our lives gives us the following perspectives:

We kill or resolve the problem

Mentally by replacing the false propaganda that has confused or mislead our opposition with a clear and compassionate truth.

Physically by activating superior skills and tactics.

Verbally by clearly broadcasting the details of other's errors in judgment, particularly those used to justify or validate harmful causes or goals.

Victory over our conflicts arises from rousing and implementing both internal and external forces making it impossible for a problem to dominate us.

We are killed or overwhelmed by the problem

Mentally when it undermines our confidence in our abilities and knowledge of things.

Physically when it degrades our nature, either slowly or rapidly, through physical abuses or excesses of any kind such as alcohol or drug abuse.

Verbally when it causes us to withdraw from communication with ourselves and others.

Any problem can destroy us if its force overwhelms either our understanding or skills necessary to stop it. The root cause of such failure is often the result of our own self-hatred or ignorance.

We evade the enemy or problem

Mentally by adopting attitudes inimical to our own and other's safety, or by refusing to acknowledge the gravity of a situation.

Physically by literally removing ourselves and others from a harmful scene.

Verbally by refusing to engage in diplomatic or placatory talks or helping to promote others to do so.

Evasion arises from a want of compassion and is a clear attempt to avoid unnecessary damage to others. It is not to be confused with denial, the refusal to accept that a problem exists.

We transform the enemy or problem

Mentally by finding and accepting mutual compromise.

Physically by declawing or neutralizing physical hostilities using superior skills and tactics.

Verbally by empathizing with another's cause when it is directed toward positive resolve.

The core ideal of Buddhist tactical philosophy is to leave no destructive wake at the outcome of any conflict but instead to turn a potentially negative situation into a positive one by striving for mutual victory. In this way, no one is left injured or maligned, only uplifted. The bully, for example, doesn't get to abuse his victim, for such victim skillfully exposes the bully's weakness in a way that offers a revelation ending the conflict in the bully's mind before it is expressed as violence thru his body. For the Buddhist masters such transformation arises from the attainment of Buddhahood.

THE MECHANICS OF MIND

"The central point of internal martial arts is mind, not Qi, as most seem to think"

Bruce K. Franzis

Understanding Mental Nature

As a career teacher I have observed that a significant degree of learning naturally occurs both unconsciously and spontaneously. Many practitioners, when given proper guidance and granted the freedom to explore, have an instinct for better body organization. But some skills acquired in their gut never rise from the visceral depths. This makes it falsely appear that there is little or no mental involvement coupled to physical action. Without digging too deeply, we can quickly see how the mind is expressed through the body. For example, on the high side of the martial spectrum we have the philosophical concept of the 'empty mind' or 'no mind' (*mushin*) a state of transcended ego. This Buddhist term refers to a quality of mind that remains after one has dissolved limiting, self-identifying, over-grasping mental tendencies. This is the part of our psyche that frequently gets in the way of our own technique when we "try too hard." Over-involving our mind can simply gum up the body's natural spontaneity. For example, we may wish to execute a technique so badly that we pay more attention to the 'desire' of getting it right or the 'fear' of getting it wrong, that we don't pay enough attention to what we are actually doing in the moment. On the low side we have mindless, misguided, irrational, inane, even insane martial behavior, which remarkably, is encouraged by some teachers. For example, one U.S. teacher would drop off his would be black belts on an urban street corner insisting they start a fight with any stranger to test their fighting skills. We need to think carefully about what we are doing, how we are doing it, and why we are doing it, as well as leaving a door open to the possibility that better methods exist. The best way to understand the role of the mind in our body, and ultimately, to balance our mental and physical natures, is to begin by observing and defining the current relationship that exists between our own mind and body.

Asian masters sought and lived with an inseparability of mind and body (a state one British scholar called *paradigmatic awareness*). Early Asian cultures themselves seemed to have experienced less mind/body splitting than their modern counterparts. Mind/heart/body was one and the same entity, like steam, water and ice. If you are an open-minded Westerner studying a martial art, consider yourself fortunate if you see your mind and body as reflections of a greater, unified self. Scientific investigation is lending more credence to the mystic's observation that our minds and bodies are the entwined threads of one organic rope designed to facilitate a synergy between the world of matter and the world of energy or spirit. Research has discovered that our human form consists of a highly expedient communications system that utilizes neurons, neuro-chemicals, light and sound waves, piezoelectric fields, proticity (energy generated from protons), electric and magnetic channels. Science is gaining headway in defining and demystifying such vitalizing forces like *Qi* as more people awaken to their own interior workings. For some of us the mystery isn't so much in naming these forces but directing them practically and effectively.

I could not have written this book without my cognitive abilities, nor successfully input the material on my keyboard without the fine motor control of my fingers. Therefore, I am happy to be both of sound mind and able body. However, let me be clear. It is not necessary for a competitor in the ring or an assault victim to verbally articulate the nuances of his martial actions in order to be victorious. It is more important for a combatant to be in the moment of physical action, rather than in the moment of reflective thought about one's response. For teachers and students, however, it is important, at least initially, to be both in the moments of thought and action in order to absorb, fully embrace, and convey the depth of the Martial Ways intelligently. The wise sensei will explain and often disentangle these subtle elements of mind for his students.

The outer characteristics of Martial Ways training have been finely dissected and well documented. We have parsed our fighting arts into the physical tools: punches, kicks, submission holds, sweeps, pressure points, energy manipulations, etc. We activate our tools with tactics; takedowns, locks, hand and leg strikes, etc. We activate our tactics with an overall strategy, an inner action set by our cognitive platform. Strategy emerges out of our character. Mental platforms are formed out of our beliefs. Our beliefs rest upon an energetic foundation of raw, intrinsic energy patterns. Our core organizations of mind are frequently set at early stages of life and solidify into habitual states of consciousness that often repeat the same choices of strategy and tactics thus creating continuous loops of failure or success. Understanding advanced technique requires that we investigate our states of mind and those raw subterranean energy flows that fuel them. Some advanced practitioners are so adept that they can clearly detect another's underlying mind/body organization before they even move! In India there was a renowned martial technique called *Iksana Vidya* that gave one the ability to assess and

direct other's thoughts or intentions. When we assemble all the inner and outer characteristics of the martial arts, we are presented with a much wider and dynamic picture of their real form.

The Many Shapes Of Form

Most every student can recall instances where their teacher corrects their physical posture or their application of a movement against a partner. Training focus and conversations abound daily in dojos about the correct 'form' of a technique. In our classes we encourage members to openly discuss the elements of proper form. I follow the dictum — know it and you claim it. During these talks, definitions of 'efficiency, fluidity, coordination, relaxation,' etc., roll easily off their tongues but, interestingly, the majority of students almost solely describe characteristics only of karate's physical or outer nature.

There is actually a five-tiered matrix to martial form that extends into different layers of reality and whose entirety makes up the full face of martial training. Many great masters worked well into the fourth and fifth layers shown below.

Each layer exerts an influence upon the layer above and below it, for there is a 'form' to the tactics or assembly of the physical tools we choose to engage our opponents with. Just as you can have poor form in a roundhouse kick, or a submission hold, you can execute a poor set of tactics, or choose a poor strategy, and so on down the line. One must therefore consider the 'form of tactics', the 'form of one's strategy', and ultimately, the 'form of mind'. If your state of mind is not wholesome then your strategies, tactics, and tools will reflect your imbalance and lead to a karma of impasses. The outcome will not be what you wished for. There are terrific martial technicians whose personalities are dysfunctional or abusive even though their arts may contain elevated practices. Skill in one layer does not presume skill or success in the others. The masters took a deep interest in the qualities that made up correct form in all five of the 'form fields' listed below.

Physical Tools: kicks, punches, locks, submissions etc.
Tactics: the organization, selection, and presentation of the tools
Strategy: the overall goal
State of Mind: one's mental platform (belief structure)
Raw, unfiltered energy patterns

Mind Matters

Simply stated, the mind matters. For the serious practitioner it merits our attention. Since it's both our mind and body that co-drive our existence it makes sense that we can gain greater insight and advance our physical skills by understanding the relationship of one to the other. According to the British author, Terrance Dukes, "We involve the body because it's easy to study the reflections of the mind in the body. The body's moment-to-moment availability frees us from having to carry around study books or consult the Internet."

Mind is also the product of the 'moving matter' that makes up our physical body. In my opinion, it is our brain/body physiology coupled to our surrounding 'environmental physiology' that produces our experience of mind.

Conversely, our physical matter is the product of our moving, 'non-physical' mind. Our fears, desires and intentions are internal currents that give shape to our body and meaning to our actions in a continuous action loop. Mind and body flow constantly into one another. A body builder develops his physique first through an active imagination that focuses on a successful outcome coupled to a strong mental desire to train. The mental catalyst activates the physical drills that lead to a highly defined physique.

This dual-reflecting, dual-actualizing, state of the mind mirroring and activating the body, and the body mirroring and activating the mind, was noted by the Asian and Indian masters. Just as the mind proved a great medium for study of the body, the body proved an equally effective medium for the study of the mind. In addition, when mind and body work in sync, like our two hands, we simply move better.

Winning Fights Versus Excelling At Martial Arts

Untrained persons lacking in martial skills or even basic intelligence have won competition matches and street encounters through sheer tenacity of will and gut alone. There are also times when victory is had by pure luck. The Universe favors us when it provides a banana peel for our assailant to slip on. On the other hand, even the most talented martial artists have gotten trounced. Consider the old joke where two men get into a scuffle? One arrogantly says "black belt" and assumes a fighting stance. The other yells "crow bar," and knocks the black belt senseless. No matter how skilled or how smart you are, the world can and often will produce your better. Winning street or competition

level fighting presents only one dimension of Martial Ways training. Asian warrior traditions grew well beyond surviving street scuffles and ring bouts. On the whole, the Martial Way fosters a deep intelligence to bring an able mind and body into harmony with itself and its surroundings, a true battle worth fighting.

Six Vital Mental Functions In Martial Arts

The mind weaves itself into our martial art through mindful practices that increase our sensitivity to our physical energies, states of mind, the bodies and states of minds of our opponents, events, and objects positioned around us. Traditional mindfulness practices consist of meditative, solo forms or kata training, and other specific integrating drills that awaken and sharpen the perceptions for making ever finer distinctions about our actions. Purely object-oriented or 'hard-goal' training has a habit of stealing the sensitivities away from our inward energy flow. This can distract us from both recognizing and activating many of our basic cognitive and energetic assets.

What are our mental assets? Suppose you lacked the ability to correctly sense your opponent's movements? Suppose you couldn't recall how to block or you miscalculated your defense? What if you couldn't maintain mental focus? Seconds count heavily in a fight. A fraction of a second error can spell defeat. The average martial artist takes for granted the neurochemical interfaces that signal us when to throw a counter punch, where the target is, or how fast it's moving.

I once watched my younger brother take a blow to the face from a belligerent friend. I saw it coming. He didn't. He hadn't had any training in how to read hostile behavioral cues. Even having a board-splitting kick or killer punch is not always enough to secure victory. Alert mind/body teamwork is needed.

Sharpening our mind offers us the best physical support. (Note: we are discussing one side of a two-sided coin purely from an academic perspective.) It is impossible to separate mental from physical actions. However, let's take a look at the primary mental functions that support our physical movements:

Perception: Our ability to draw accurate data from the world around and inside us. Three different types of perceptive apparatus are at our disposal.

Proprioception gives us the ability to know where parts of our body are in relationship to each other through muscular, tendon and articular sources.

Exteroception gives us the ability to draw information from outside the body through the six 'exteroceptor' sense organs; sight, smell, taste, touch, hearing, and balance.

Interoception gives us the ability to draw information about our internal organs.

Logic gives us the ability to orderly sift through the information collected above to determine for example, the degree of threat, where the threat is, how it is motioning etc. which then allows us to select appropriate body tools.

Intuition gives us the ability to draw from non-logical, non-linear knowledge on how to maximize our response. Intuition is the wellspring of spiritual sensitivity. Intuition also represents our degree of sensitivity to Qi (intrinsic energy). Because the awareness of Subtle Energy is not a cultural goal, very little is spoken about it in Western societies.

Memory gives us the ability to recall past events, their values, and a perspective on how to best use our tools to respond.

Intention directs mental and physical energy to activate our martial tools.

Concentration holds our physical actions to a conclusion.

These six mental tools, along with our hardwired gut instincts, guide us in choosing when, where, why and how to initiate a physical motion. If any these faculties are underdeveloped or impaired we may not get too far in our endeavors.

Whether we are physically still or moving, our Qi is streaming and 'communicating' with other energies in proximity, including our opponent's Qi or energy field. How do we understand how Qi communicates if it has no mouth, eyes, or ears? We do so by way of our sensitivity and self-awareness. Simply being sensitive does not mean you are aware of the data coming to you. Advanced internal martial artists not only train to become aware of Qi but learn to differentiate amongst Qi's three general reactions on the body/mind complex. Qi will always exert degrees of Positive/Promoting, Neutral/Balancing or Negative/Sedating influence. Positive energy in and around us adds to our vitality and strength. It fortifies our body and mind and subsequently our martial techniques. Negative/Sedating energy diminishes us both physically and mentally. Neutral/Balancing energy neither adds to nor depletes us in any appreciable manner but rather holds us to a constancy of being. The more sensitive a practitioner becomes, the keener his assessment and accessibility of these flowing energies. Developing a sensitivity gauge, learning how to discriminate degrees of influences is a critical part of internal martial arts training.

For those coming from of a purely Hard style orientation this subject will reveal a hidden *art within your art*. Your choice to pay attention to subtle energies or not does not erase their existence. Once you discover and activate them they will become a vital asset to your martial repertoire.

Why There Is Little Talk About The Mind's Role In Martial Arts

There appears little agreement amongst the world's martial teachers as to what aspects of the mind, if any, ought to be valued. Ancient practices, which taught layered and complex body/mind principles, splintered during the forward march of human evolution, leaving us with compartmentalized skills in the form of tournament specialists, pressure point specialists, self-defense specialists, kata specialists, ground-grappling experts, etc. Today's 'Hard Style' teachers prove highly adept at conveying the biomechanical side of their technique but too often hold overly simplistic views of the mind's influence upon these techniques or just fail to address them altogether.

By understanding how our mind interfaces with the body we can activate much finer layers to our martial actions. Lacking this knowledge excludes many practitioners from grasping or using advanced principles. Mindless martial action fixes practitioners in the animal realm. We may still fight ferociously, even victoriously, while out of our minds, but pure primal engagements strip us of our moral and compassionate compass and do not allow us to leverage broader remedies and skills.

Although it may feel like our mind has vacated once things get down and dirty, it is still very much involved in our doings. A long-standing characteristic of the mind is to speak its wisdom thru the physical body. This behind-the-scene role of the psyche can easily be likened to a field general on a hill assessing and directing his infantry below. The mind observes and calculates from its bunkered cranial lookout in constant communication with its material troops through an ultra fast/ultra complex network of command and control biocircuitry.

OPENING THE BRAIN DOOR

"In the Speed of Fight
Animate moves faster than inanimate.
Mind moves faster than body.
Spirit moves faster than mind."

To better understand the mind's connection to our martial technique it's helpful to open up, what one student creatively called, the "Brain Door." The brain door opens when we can:

Distinguish between our biomechanical, psychic, and soft-wired energetic bodies

Distinguish between consciousness and unconsciousness

Distinguish Right from Left Brain influences and characteristics

Distinguish three states of mind: Common Mind, Uncommon Mind, and Quantum Mind.

Biomechanical Body vs. Psychic Body vs. Energetic Body:

The **Biomechanical Body** refers to our musculoskeletal leveraging and weight distributing system, the end point of our mental intentions. The physical body is essentially our mind's root into matter. When a stimulus triggers our intention, that intent is sent along nerve and meridian pathways to activate the muscles that leverage our response to the outside world. This biomechanical system uses all our connective tissue structures: muscles, tendons, fascia and ligament, cartilage etc., to extend and contract our limbs, balance us, pull us through space or punch thru our opponents. No matter how hard we think, it is ultimately our fleshy fist and foot that thumps into the heavy bag, not the glob of grey matter percolating in our skulls. Mind acts the trigger. Body the bullet. Mind is the General, Body the infantry. We want our infantry conditioned, strong, and responsive. Drilling the correct physical form strengthens the neural communication between mind and body increasing the body's caliber of performance.

The term **Psychic Body** generally refers to our thinking and intending mind, the mental form that weighs our actions through the combined efforts of intellect and intuition before we implement them. For Westerners, Mind is Central Command. The ancient Greeks coined the word *Psyche* for a mysterious force, which they believed entered the living. Just as breathing can be considered the medium between our physical and emotional body, our mental body can be viewed as a bridge or medium mysteriously entering our physical and Energetic Body. Weighing issues before acting upon them can be extremely helpful. Being able to clearly logic or intuit the variables of a conflict gives us a tactical edge.

The term **Energy Body** (or Mind/QI form) refers to the streaming energies of our neural and perineural complex. We are all composed of electro-magnetic, hormonal, piezoelectric, chemical, thermal, aural (sound) and photonic (light-motivated), gravity and elastic energies operating under and

PART 2

beyond the skin, generating a dynamic charged atmosphere around us. In the West we refer to these forces as Subtle Energy and the surrounding etheric energy ball encasing us as an aura or auric field. Asian masters felt that this invisible "second body," or what the Indian Buddhists called the *Vajra* Body, could be cultivated and then mentally directed to amplify any action. But this control required an acute sensitivity to its currents along with consistent practice. With repeated focus on specific movement patterns combined with precise mental visualizations and respiratory actions, anyone could activate these currents further brought to light by specific *shime* (tests) given by the masters to direct one's attention to them (the Okinawan kata, *Sanchin*, is one of these energy-sensitizing patterns.) Okinawan masters would test their disciple's Qi placement by striking specific muscle groups where the Qi was pooling. Modern students can cultivate and direct their Energy Bodies to reinforce their musculoskeletal actions with the aid of forms like Sanchin.

Through internal practices we are seeking to elevate our knowledge and organizational level of what Buddhists call the *Sanmitsu*, or Three Mysteries of Mind, Body, and Speech—literally, the vibes that come out of our mouths, (figuratively, the vibes that all things give off) so that they may move in accord. Although we commonly think that the mind projects its desire through bodily action in a linear, cause and effect manner, such as, "I think, therefore I act," the Buddhist kempo masters believe that we 'think/act' simultaneously (in the sense that the moment we intend, our Energy Body springs into action with electrochemical effect). However, our culture has become so fixated, so habituated, to the surface actions of our mind that we don't see the simultaneity of these events. As a result we work within a narrow reality band that creates the illusion of a technique's linearity. The truth is that a fight or conflict begins well before the first strike is ever thrown. An unseen energy battle is already underway before the actual fur flies.

Conscious vs. Unconscious

The mind is a vessel of ever-shifting awareness and continuity. One minute we acutely feel our heart throbbing. The next moment our pulse is lost in friendly conversation. Suddenly, the conversation sours and we are lunging at each other's throats spurred on by an intense cascade of angry, neuro-chemical, hormone-driven rage that drowns out all our daily concerns.

Consciousness (awareness) refers to our fluctuating states of mental lucidity. Sometimes we are self-aware and sometimes we are not. In one moment our mind can have razor sharp focus. We know

71

exactly where our big left toe is pointing and why it's pointing that way. The next moment, adrift in thought, we bang our head into the bathroom door. Like respiration, consciousness has both a voluntary and involuntary quality. We are present at some facets of our reality while absent from others. With respiration we can hold our breath, loose our breath, or forcefully exhale. With consciousness we can voluntarily focus our mind inwardly or outwardly, let our awareness freely roam or switch off our attention. Insight into this variable characteristic of consciousness will help you frame better responses to conflicted situations.

The Japanese refer to types of insight as *ken*. The solo nature of kata practice develops a particular type of insight into one's own being called *Jiken*. Kumite, or the 'free exchange' with others develops *Taken*—insight into another's being. Both kata and kumite become indispensable actions likened to our right and left hands. Each works uniquely to pierce fictions of the ego, induce harmony, and develop the only form of confidence worth attaining. Achieving a high degree of Jiken and Taken results in a state of 'flowing insight' termed *Naiken*. Both categories develop mindfulness, increase mental flexibility, and expand the consciousness. As we practice to open ourselves to new ideas and new ways of moving we enhance our adaptability to the world at large.

I refer to the **Unconscious** as our subliminal awareness. One part of us is able to sense under the radar of another part. Our senses absorb a far greater quantity of data than our self-identifying egos understand. While unconscious, our mind appears to be directed by forces both outside of our control or awareness. This 'Universal' or 'Source Mind' occasionally borrows our energy by putting our self-consciousness into sleep mode for purposes we don't yet fully comprehend.

While intellect provides us with the power of emotionless, cool calculation, intuition opens the doorway between the conscious and unconscious mind. We can widen this doorway thru quiet meditative moments and by tuning into our feelings instead of always 'thinking' them thru. We can also gain from moments of Left Brain detachment, as you will read about. Some Mystics suggest that it's not a bad idea to let the universe steer us once in a while.

Right Brain Versus Left Brain

The human brain is a two-for-one organ. Two distinct hemispheres of brain matter sit in our skulls functioning in two completely different manners. Place your two fists side by side, thumbs facing you. This is roughly what your brain hemispheres look like in your skull. These two brains communicate with one another through a thick neural network called the *corpus collosum*. Interestingly, the right side of your body is hotwired to the left side of your brain and vice versa. The way these two brains interact forms our personalities.

An EEG (electro-encephalogram) records the electrical activity of our brain's hemispheres. Broad research reveals that the majority of us show the greatest electrical activity in our left hemisphere, considered the location for most analytical, logic-based thinking. Our right hemisphere, by contrast, is more concerned with sensing the larger picture. Even though brain activity switches quickly between the hemispheres from moment to moment, brain experiments in the 1970's revealed that up to ninety-five percent of society fits a functional map of verbal and nonverbal thinking, represented in separate left and right brain activities. The left brain generally dominates our mental activity and is reinforced by formal education. Most U.S. educational institutions place a higher value on Left brain skills like mathematics, logic, and language than on the Right brain functions like intuition and imagination.

Left Brain

Our brain's left hemisphere is analytical, sequential, verbal, practical, rooted in reality and detail, objective and logical. It deals with language, interpretation, categorization, cause and effect relationships, writing, science and math. This "male" brain is assertive, aggressive and authoritative. The left hemisphere is stimulated by informational input but enters 'sleep mode' during meditation or in sensory-deprived surroundings allowing the right brain to fill our minds with emotional and visual imagery. Most Western civilizations are considered Left brain cultures because they continually reinforce and reassert logic-dominating functions.

Right Brain

The right brain concerns itself with the big picture. This hemisphere is subjective, intuitive, visual, imaginative, emotional, free of time restraint and spontaneous. It deals with symbols and imagery, philosophy, religion, physical activity, spatial relationship of shape, color, and pattern, art, rhythm, music and dance. This "female" or Yin brain is emotional, passive, creative and holistic. Right-brain individuals tend to be calmer and less stressed about life. The right hemisphere is also responsible for movement, especially automatic movement.

Enter Martial Arts

The early kempo masters were not modern neuroscientists, yet they unwittingly intuited that a balanced brain led to a balanced life. Their meditative practices toned down or switched off Left brain chatter, allowing the right side to exercise its creative, spontaneous, and intuitive flow. Whole brain thinking, if not the prime objective of temple-based martial disciplines, was certainly a critical part of its foundation.

During the 1980's I was tested on a sophisticated biofeedback machine by a Manhattan, New School neurophysicist. She told me that my brain was unusually balanced in electrical activity, likely as a direct result of my martial practices.

Science also tells us that physical activity itself makes us more right-brained. Due to the brain's amazing plasticity, repetitive physical actions build new neural connections so that such tasks can be performed effortlessly, without thought—without trying. Advanced martial artists don't "think" about their movements. They perform automatically, without mental restraint.

Many Eastern spiritual and physical disciplines, like the martial arts, noted that calming the mind enhanced self-awareness, which led to more effective responses. Perhaps, in this light, Eastern and Western culture act as a metaphor for the Right and Left Brain functions.

Intelligence is not the sole providence of the mind or body, or of one brain sphere over the other. Moving the body is moving the mind. By balancing our mental and physical activity we not only enhance our overall effectiveness but we also integrate the best of our two brain worlds – the world of logic, strategy, and analysis, and its complimentary world of Subtle Energy, and the perspective of the wholeness and interconnectedness of life.

Our Western habituation with its left-brained traits of individuality, analytical thinking, and empirical knowledge, is certainly of great value but it has also made it difficult for much of our society to shut off an incessant inner and often divisive chatter, or to break our skepticisms regarding the existence or value of subtle energies. Some Eastern disciplines offer us a brain-balancing option. They encourage community, holistic and intuitive thinking, and Subtle Energy awareness. Knowing the differences that occur between Left or Right brain dominance offers us an explanation of why some martial artists are attracted to meditation and inward directed practices, while others just don't get it. As one author stated, "You simply cannot grasp holism through non-holistic means." Developing the holistic right brain is a key to experiencing an enhanced dimension to martial practice.

The Triple Layered Mind

I use the concept of a triple-layered mind to distinguish between three tiers of mental functioning that draw from our Right and Left brain hemispheres. I refer to these three attributes of consciousness as the Common, Uncommon, and Quantum Mind fields. Although each of us, in truth, possess the capacity to command a wide mental frontier in how and what we receive and transmit, we always have the choice:

1. to stay in common mental territory, that is, to confine or tune our thinking to what is generally known by us and those around us.

2. to tune into an uncommon mental field of what others have discovered but which we ourselves do not presently know.

3. To tune into or venture into completely unexplored mental wilderness unknown even by the majority of the educated populace.

We could analogize a mind moving within these three vibratory fields to a radio with the dial acting as our intention or station chooser. Commonly trod mental ground can be likened to a single, familiar radio station: the broader but marked fields, as the entire range of man made radio stations, and lastly, the unexplored mental wilderness as 'Universal stations,' that is, off the chart of general human awareness.

A Radio is defined by its bandwidth. Most radio bandwidths range from 3 Hz (hertz) to 300 GHz (Gigahertz). A hertz is a vibration measured in oscillations per second. One Hertz equals one vibration per second. One MHz equals one million Hertz per second. A radio essentially transmits information (and energy) through these oscillations. We interpret these 'waves' through our own sensory apparatus, which converts them into electrical transmissions in our brain, which then decodes them into what we interpret as news or entertainment by way of sound and images, because every organ in our body vibrates like a transmitter and receiver. By tuning into a radio station we intermingle our energy waves with the radio's airwaves. Consider your martial pursuits with this analogy in mind.

Mental Setting 1 We move only between a fixed bandwidth say from 90 to 100FM. This limited scope defines the Common Mind. Common mental functioning sticks to its favorite channels and rarely, if ever, explores other stations. In martial arts we can liken this to a student who exclusively favors a particular kick or punch and never expands his striking inventory beyond a few techniques.

Mental Setting 2 We roam across the entire bandwidth of the human-made radio wave spectrum.

This expanded freedom describes the movement of our Uncommon Mind. This mind taps into the flow of all man-made knowledge simply by broadening the focus of attention. Hundreds of potentially new martial techniques open to us as we share our ideas and search multi-media avenues for more information.

Mental Setting 3 We extend our listening ability beyond the man-made radio bandwidth to pull in universe-generated stations. With specialized training we can catch, decode, and make sense of even finer vibrations in the Quantum universe. This 'beyond the man-made' radio bandwidth is analogous to a mind with limitless potential and sensitivity. As our sensitivity increases, our Quantum Mind picks up increasingly more refined waves of information and energy. Ancient cultures referred to these universe-generated stations as the spirit, mantric, or vibrational world. The art of tuning into this invisible world is described as spiritual practice. Not only can we receive from this vast field of energy but we can also project our own energies into it. By developing martial techniques that use shifts in the body's Subtle Energy fields we can advantage ourselves with high-end tactics often completely unaware to our opposition. Consider the example in the chapter, *The Mystery of Power* at the beginning of this book in which Ralph demonstrates his iron palm to an unbelieving fellow student.

The Seven Chakras With Their Corresponding Brain Wave Frequencies

Let's digress from mainstream martial thinking for a moment and take a brief look at the Indian Hindu yogic concept of the Chakras for another viewpoint on the mind's root in the physical body to add further insight into internal martial practice.

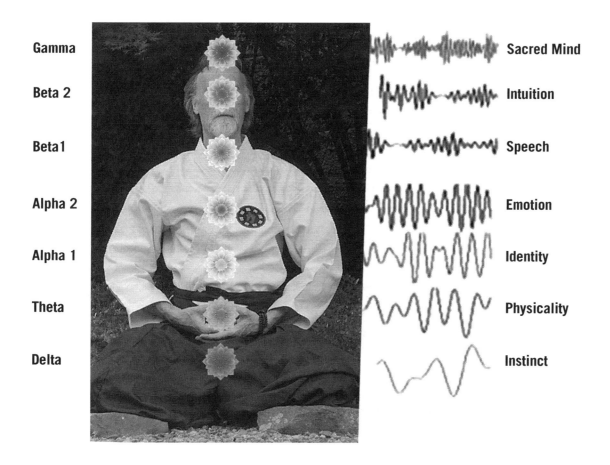

Gamma — Sacred Mind

Beta 2 — Intuition

Beta 1 — Speech

Alpha 2 — Emotion

Alpha 1 — Identity

Theta — Physicality

Delta — Instinct

The Relevance Of The Hindu Spiritual Chakric System
On The Practice Of Martial Arts

Some historians trace our martial origins to ancient India where the Hindu yogic systems utilized a concept of energy flow called the *Chakras* whose development reaches back 2,500 years. The Chakra system adds further evidence of an existing energy matrix separate from the generally accepted neural, brain-to-body communications loop. For centuries, Indian Yogi's have taught that the body consists of seven primary energy vortices found on the front and corresponding back of every human. These centers are said to transfer vital life force to and from the body. The word *chakra* means 'wheel' and its implication is that each of these wheels spin intrinsic energy (Qi) into and out of us. Each wheel is stacked in a column and connected to major nerve ganglia that branch out from our spine and major endrocrine glands.

The seven chakras are found along the spinal cord from the perineum (base of the spine) to the top of the head. What I find intriguing about the chakras is that each of them correlate to various states of consciousness that begin in the lower three chakras with our animal instincts and ascend upward into our intellectual and compassionate energy fields. Each chakra has a specific psychological representation or reference. That is, we can define the functioning of each chakra in terms of their effects upon our psyche. The yogis realized that not only did specific *asana* (postures) affect the body's physiology, but by altering the mind, one could just as powerfully adjust the bodily chakras. They witnessed a well-defined top/down and bottom/up synergy of unconventional forces at work in their practices.

The point of this diagram is simply to portray the intimate interconnectedness of mind/body communication and to show that our mind is deeply embedded in our body just as our body is deeply embedded in our mind. You cannot affect one state without touching the other. And to take this idea one step further, if you enhance your mental capacity, you can increase your physical strength and thus improve the outcome of any action.

In martial arts, higher levels of information and energy become accessible by tuning into the chakric frequencies through specifically patterned movement sequences, visualizations, meditations and breathing practices. These variables became part of an inner kata training meant to compliment its outer format. However, this inner manual was not transmitted to most early American practitioners returning from Okinawa, Korea, and Japan.

Tuning into these higher 'quantum' frequencies unpacks greater information and energy resources allowing individuals to accomplish unusual feats like some of those mentioned on the back of this book. Let's now distinguish amongst the three mindsets to help us better navigate through our martial practices.

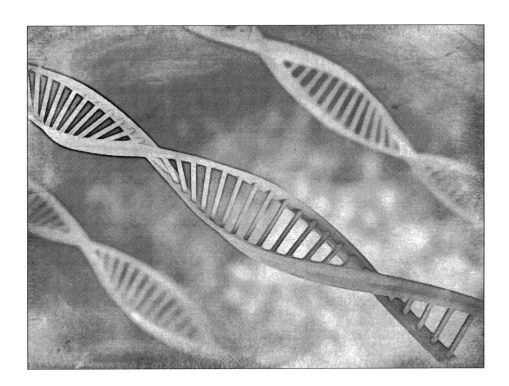

**The double helix could just as easily be a representation
of the interdependency of mind and body or of the Hard and Soft
aspects of martial training**

The Common Mind
I maul

Common Mind refers to our everyday, base, and instinctive mental functioning. This is the part of our mind that attends to all repetitive daily actions; dressing, brushing our teeth, cooking, sleeping, eating, shopping, driving, sitting, breathing etc., and also to our most basic repetitive dojo drills like stretching, punching, kicking and blocking. We could also call the Common Mind, the ordinary, or workhorse mind.

The Common Mind's bandwidth is anchored to gross or visceral reality, not far removed from animal behavior. Therefore we could view the Common Mind as an animal-cultured, animal-anchored or preset, instinctive mind. This mind quickly embraces a 'what you see is what you get' world.

Common Mind thinking follows linear, cause and effect rules of engagement. An example of Com-

80

mon Mind activity might be the way 17th century generals commanded their armies to amass across from one another and fire volleys point blank into their adversary's ranks. Today such a tactic would be considered a gross waste of human life, but it was the best strategy for its time. Consider that such a battle plan was initiated by a *state of mind.*

When threatened, our Common Mind activates our vocal chords to bark menacingly, our face to contort and bare its teeth. If we must fight, the Common Mind wants to immediately and aggressively maul, bludgeon, or pummel the threat.

The Common Mind's command center is located in the 500 million year old, instinct-driven, Reptilian system or brain stem, the oldest part of the human brain complex. This Hindbrain connects to the spinal cord and controls our most basic life processes. The Reptilian brain regulates blood pressure, breathing and the basest of activities toward power, material needs, and physical pleasures. The conquest of food, sex, etc. draws and exercises this part of the brain. Its field outpost, or material 'root' in the body, is defined by the gurus of India as the lower chakras. The Common Mind activates its physical power system to satisfy its basic interests from the three lower Chakras.

The sages tell us our Common Mind, though highly functional (like a screwdriver), is only the ambassador of our surface reality. We all innately possess a higher faculty. In the authenticating dojo we discover the mind's higher workings.

What Are Some Martial Implications Of The Common Mind Practice?

The Common Mind relies primarily on its primitive and animalistic wiring to carry the body through danger. From the martial perspective, when there is no escape from a threat, the Common Mind immediately activates the instinctive, reactive, *gut* warrior, what our dojo calls the *Red Man*. At this level of response one's technique is executed in a semi or unconscious manner. A little knowledge becomes a dangerous expression when you give someone a rudimentary grasp of martial technique and they find themselves in an intense exchange. I once observed a kumite between two fierce, intermediate-skilled students rapidly degrade into a wild, hair-pulling brawl. Technical finesse was thrown out the window. In another match, one student got so worked up that he delivered a full force chop to his partner's neck. The instructors stood aghast, unable to stop him, as his *shuto* crashed down without any inhibition or care for his training partner's safety. He had been overcome by his primitive drive for self-preservation. At that moment he was utterly out of his mind.

The Uncommon Mind
I box

The Uncommon Mind is the *educated* mind. Education derives from the Latin word *educaree*, meaning *to draw from*. Education allows us to draw from civilization's or nature's knowledge bank, rather than solely from our own gut wiring as to how and why things work. Education connects the dots between ideas, actions, events, history, and the placement and patterns of matter in order to gain broader understanding and accomplishment. Education is not limited solely to the institutionalized academic teachings of high schools, colleges and karate dojos. It includes the School of Hard Knocks, for the every day world can prove as effective a teacher as any Ivy League setting. The Uncommon Mind is less restricted because of its ability to dwell in the conceptual or abstract, which gives it a premeditated tactical advantage over the Common Mind. The Uncommon Mind can be thought of as the ambassador of reality's substrata or deeper realms.

However, even an educated mind can fall prey to a 'what you are told, or what you tell yourself, is what you see' world. For education sometimes encourages the wrong outcome, assessment, or conclusion. Remember, the world was once staunchly believed to be flat.

I suspect the Uncommon Mind is linked to the Medulla Oblongata or Mammalian brain. Scientists estimate this part of the brain was formed about 300 million years ago. It is fueled by the three upper torso and head chakras. Activating these upper chakras opens and channels our compassion to flow, but even within the Uncommon Mind, prejudice or bias can exist, narrowing our compassion to an immediate circle of family, community, or tribe while shunning outsiders as the unprivileged.

When directed toward self-protection, the educated mind avails itself of specialized tools and tactics. Its defining warrior cry is "I Box," contrary to the blunt, traumatizing bestial actions of the Common Mind. Education gives us more efficient tactics and tools and thus more precision to ensure a greater chance of success. This mind understands that, "If I hone, I can fight intelligently." The martial arts awaken the Uncommon Mind by providing effective combative skills and insight into the nature of physical conflict. This is why martial arts reign as the world's most effective, individual, unarmed, civil protection systems.

The Quantum Mind
I Merge

Quantum Mind seems an appropriate contemporary term to describe a cosmic or quantum-generated mind. This is a mind sensitive to and in sync with what we could call the 20th century's, "quantum culture." The word *quantum* comes from the Latin word *quantus*, meaning 'how much.' Quantum Physics is a branch of physics that describes the properties of a physical system. In Quantum Physics, the word *Quantum* refers to a discrete quantity of electromagnetic radiation. No mysticism is intended by this description if we apply it to the human system. This simply means that outside influences; obvious ones like career changes, social relationships, temperature, terrain—the ten thousand doings of the universe, and those not so obvious ones like planetary shifts, sunspots, topographical arrangements etc., also influence and/or activate/supress our behaviors. The Quantum Mind is merged with, fueled by, and tuned into this subtle confluence of forces surrounding and engulfing us. Because this mindset operates along the widest bandwidth, the Quantum Mind is capable of the highest level of interaction. This is the mental state tapped into by the spiritual masters.

INTERNAL KARATE

The Quantum Mind is free of restrictive cultural beliefs and attitudes. Divested of unhealthy, disintegrating ego obstructions, and functioning at an ultra-sensitive level, our Quantum Mind lets us cast into a sea of vast possibilities, transcendentalisms, what ifs and why nots. Consider the Quantum Mind as the ambassador of the Unlimited. This mind is the playground of the masters. The Quantum Mind grasps that 'what you do not see is also what you get.' It senses patterns within previously hidden patterns and lets one adapt to and use the insights. The Quantum Mind embraces an expansive community, one that is not solely people-oriented. A mind that uses this expansive community as an extension of itself becomes far more potent than one using a Common mindset.

I suspect that we will discover that the Quantum Mind draws its mental power from the outermost brain called the neo-cortex or frontal lobe that formed about 4 million years ago. It is fueled by the spiritual or crown chakra on top of the head. The Quantum Mind dissolves the obstructing distinctions of 'I' as an entity solely encased in skin. It removes the filters between a separate outside and inside reality. The Quantum Mind joins these two domains into one unified field of being and action, dissolving the duality of a 'you' and a 'they.' This is why the spiritual masters say that the mind (specifically, our self-identifying ego), and the opponent, are one and the same. If you 'kill' the ego you vanquish the opponent, for no mind equals no conflict. All that remains is One.

Unlike the Common Mind's attachment to the world as an 'I' to an 'it', the Quantum Mind offers less or no 'I' to attach itself. Because this mind possesses a filter from distracting self-interests, it is free to react and to receive unconditionally. Depersonalized, it perceives no enemies, only obstacles. This is the mind-set of the great masters of the *Do*.

The art of fighting to transcend fighting becomes accomplished only in this inner field. This mindset is evident in all people who have sought and achieved this goal. From the Hindu chakric perspective the *Do* is achieved when the crown chakra is fully opened and balanced with all the other chakras of the body.

Moving From One Mind Set To Another

Human feeling is not a fixed entity. These mindsets describe varying degrees of sensitivity and self-awareness. Some days we are just more attuned to things. Most of us however, reveal a general habitation in one mental pasture over another. Spiritual practice shifts the mental framework toward Quantum Mind sensitivity.

As one advances through the Common, Uncommon, and Quantum sensitivities they will experience a gradual self-expansion, inner calmness, and greater sense of self-organization. This broadening also gives one the ability to detect and/or decode finer patterns of activity and energy around them. Common Mind sensitivity sees only the immediately visible life and its need for safety and survival in it; the need to eat, to shelter, to cloth. This bare-necessity mental functioning values efficiency, as it gets right to the obvious point of the matter. It reacts simply and directly; I see a bridge, a friend, a foe. I must eliminate this and add that. But its restrictive scope can also set our behaviors to act in exclusive or harmful ways. For example, I witnessed a free-style kumite in which one man accidentally hit another (not an uncommon occurrence), until the man hit retaliated in an impulsive, eye-for-an-eye exchange that ultimately sent his partner to the hospital. His was a base response. He felt hurt and decided to hurt back to balance the event.

Uncommon (educated) sensitivities will grasp more subtle patterns behind the obvious and immediate visible actions. Education helps us to see through the veil of the surface world. For example, with a heightened sensitivity we might recognize that our competitor's overly aggressive action

against us has its origins in anger coming from a past incident unrelated to our current exchange. If so, we may not take such hostility personally. Animals, unlike us, do not seem to possess the faculty to weigh or contemplate pre or post events.

The Quantum sensitivities present us with unfiltered, unconditional, raw reality. There are masters who can feel an opponent's mental organization to throw a punch well before the opponent's body has given any visual clues. This is a highly intuitive mindset that picks up on very fine vibrations and can quickly and accurately decode them into useful information.

Prompts That Change Our Mind

What prompts might cause us to enter these other mental dimensions? People will generally seek a change of mind if they are suffering from failure(s) or uncomfortable disorganizations of self, and their current thinking or actions do not reduce their oppositions or mounting conflicts. They could feel opposed or repressed due to inside or outside forces. Or, they may simply have a deep and intuitive destiny, desire, or calling to explore and expand and thus seek greater leverage to move thru life.

Noting that we move between degrees of desire and resistance, Buddhist Kempo masters sought the path of least resistance, a way to move through life with minimal friction. The monastic masters recognized that not all remedies could be found in a single, one-dimensional response. Some resolutions require pulling from the universal environment to reap better information and tools.

Each of the above mindsets themselves are subjected to the five base movements described earlier: Soul death, Moving toward darkness, Holding the middle ground, Moving toward the light, Bliss. Consider also that people can compartmentalize their mindsets. For example, you could be having Common Mind behavior toward your career but Uncommon Mind actions toward your hobbies, or Quantum Mind attitudes toward your relationships. The variables can be quite complex. Because of this complexity, various disciplines emerged to resolve the discordances. Solving community-versus-community divides birthed resolution politics. Unresolved cultural, resource, and boundary hostilities gave rise to military arts; violent civilian issues birthed martial arts. Man-versus-self, i.e., our search for life's meaning and reconciliation of our mortality, grew into philosophical and religious institutions. Man versus injury, illness and mortality created our medical arts. Man-versus-community and man versus wife or family activated the social and psychological arts. Each discipline helps us to mend various rifts, address concerns and dissatisfactions in our desiring lives. All these disciplines emerged to help us cope and/or to make sense of life's uncertainties, to define its insidious conflicts and to heal or reclaim lost, repressed or damaged human territory.

Living within, becoming more aware of, or achieving any of the three functional mind depths cannot guarantee success or failure in your life or on the dojo mat. Common Mind actions can move a student toward descent as equally as ascent. The Uncommon/educated Mind can vacillate between good or evil, advance or retreat. We've read about a great many 'smart' people and institutions that have made horribly dumb decisions. Your Quantum Mind could be moving you equally toward destructive behaviors as toward constructive ones. The degree of awareness, sensitivity, or understanding that comes with each mindset is neither good nor bad. It is how we apply our degrees of awareness and the course we set upon that determines the outcome, relevancy, and value. Why we move in any direction on our awareness continuum is part of a larger karmic truth. We must also remember that our karmas (actions) are also frequently changed by proximities to other karmas. In Buddhist Kempo practice we are continually challenged to live for the greater good of the world.

Levels Of Mind Behind Martial Technique

We should seek to root and balance in all three mental states as part of our legacy as humans. It is also equally important that we ask about the level of our teacher's mind to see where our training is headed. Brains may be remarkably similar when placed in a vat of formaldehyde, but the productions of our living brains, and the purposes for which we use them, are widely divergent, and continuously uplifting or downgrading our existence. All martial performances reveal states of a Common, Uncommon and Quantum activity. When we plug into a teacher we enter the 'current' of his or her mentorship. Such a decision should not be made lightly.

The lowest mental setting of the Common Mind would be a person functioning close to animal viscerality. Martial teachers at their worst have been known to yell at, demean, deride, condescend and even beat up their students. Students at their worse behavior have been known to self-abuse; deny their body signals, push until they throw up, or punish lower level students as part of a hen-pecking hierarchy. The basest of humans are barely sentient, impulse and instinct-driven.

On the Quantum end of the spectrum we have the transcendent mental qualities. This mind field is achieved or entered when the tenant (ego) yields to its universal owner. At is zenith, the Quantum Mind is a state of mindless mind, what the Buddhist's call *mushin* – an "empty" or no mind state.

This is a mind empty of the restraints of the common or uncommon self. It is absent of "fatty chatter." The vacuity of the universe fills its domain. The Quantum Mind not only provides an elevated view of life, it lets us live wide.

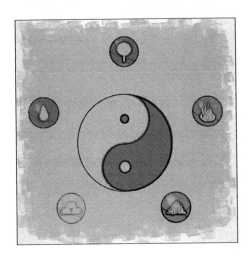

The Importance Of Polarity

Throughout this book I have established the tight interweave of body/mind principles factored into both ancient and modern higher end martial art systems. The concept of Polarity is a pre-eminent principle.

Polarity is the state of having two opposite aspects. Chinese martial arts express Polarity as Yin/Yang Theory. This theory sees us continually subjected to the forces of two compelling poles. Like the two-faced coin analogy given earlier, one can find either complementary or opposition between the coin's two sides or poles. Good versus bad, or disease versus health, implies opposition. Night and day—complementary. The principle of Polarity brings up the familiar 'cup half-empty/cup half-filled' *koan*. This mind puzzle suggests that there is more than one way to regard polarity's effects. From a physical reality, one pole pulls us toward health and self-preservation, hence the desire to learn protective skills. From the psychological perspective one pole could also be considered centric. It causes our sensitivities to develop into a "what's in it for *me* mentality." Too strong of a centric pole pulls us into an ever-condensing, self-centeredness that disregards the needs of others. As an astrological phenomenon, the centric pole could be related to a Black hole which astronomers tells us draws and condenses matter, or symbolically, as the Yin/black fish.

The physical counter-pole pulls us toward disorganization, disease and death. The psychological counter-pole is de-centric. It draws us toward communal and compassionate embrace. This pole is embodied in the statement, "How can I extend myself to others?" As an astrological phenomenon it can be viewed as the matter-spewing White Hole, or in Chinese symbolism, as the Yang/white fish. It encourages an egoless or 'less ego is more, less ego is better', mind set. This is the spiritual orientation sought after by martial monastics.

Yin and yang polarity is also reflected in the science of a magnetic dipole which is a pair of equal and opposite magnetic poles or electric charges separated by a distance. A magnetic dipole generates a magnetic field from two opposite points, as in a magnet's north and south, or, in the example of an electric dipole, a positive and a negative charge. One pole exerts and one pole receives the exertion. In Chinese thinking, the Yang pole acts—the Yin pole receives. Our own energy fields mimic the properties of electro-magnetic fields. This is why internal martial artists have studied these subtle forces in depth. In today's karate systems we can see intriguing and specific terminology that points directly to these intrinsic pole forces in the use of the martial terms *tori* and *uke*. The *tori* is the 'giver/sender' of a technique and the *uke*, the 'receiver' of that technique. These terms strongly suggest that an energy transfer is taking place beyond the observable act of one man 'giving/throwing' his physical punch to the 'taker/target'. What is also being 'given' is the energy field ahead of the physical punch, something that can be 'taken' from the attacker.

The development of Yin/Yang Theory also possesses a corollary called the Five Element or Five Phases Theory. The noted Five Elements; metal, earth, fire, water, and wood play an integral part in both Chinese martial thought and technique. This concept of interacting elements/phases refers to various subtle forces operating behind the obvious flesh and blood technique. Whether it is our aim to smash the opponent to smithereens or to quell violence with compassion, these forces distinguish a class of 'meta-skills' for halting our oppositions. The Yin/Yang and Five Element Theories proved so compelling that the Chinese templated them into their medical practices, which sought to balance yin/yang forces in the body, and into their manipulation of the exterior environment, found in the art of *Feng Shui*, to harmonize people with the forces in nature. And so, the enlightened martial artist

becomes one who strives for a state of balance within a constant flow of human/earth/and cosmic energy fields.

Where you 'locate' or 'center' your mind determines how much pull each pole will exert. Our location or point of view within the material and mental world fixes us somewhere between the two "floating" pole worlds. I call them "floating" because the forces they exert and our proximity to them are constantly shifting. Everything animate and inanimate floats, bumps, and rubs one another in an infinite and changing energy sea that is continuously influencing and being influenced.

Each of the three mindsets described above is capable of fulfilling various divides. The Common Mind is adept at filling our gut/material pleasures like food, clothing, shelter, sexual needs and power. The Uncommon Mind satisfies our palate for intellectual/conceptual pleasures. This is the need to continually grow and to know how and why things work. The Quantum Mind tackles the big questions: reunion with our higher self, the Source-That-Knows-No-Limit, God, Universal Mind or whatever one chooses to call the greatness surrounding us. The Quantum Mind fills our devotional pleasures and existential curiosities.

All the martial artists of the world are training with different mental involvements expressed through their bodies. Our muscles are not all getting the same juice. We are not all punching from the same mental platforms or perspectives. We do not all display the same currency of being and therefore do not express the same focus even if our actions appear identical on the physical plane. Some of us are punching empty space to survive. Others, punch to beat up the ghosts of past abusers. Some are punching to win a future competition or to prove their self-worth. Others are punching to thrive. Some of us are throwing small shovels of dirt into our divides while others are bulldozing their gaps with gigantic, mind/body team effort.

Now that we have taken a close look at and established the intimate relationship of the mind's influence on the body, let's distinguish our warrior powers.

PART 3
WARRIOR POWER

If you do not believe, it cannot be. If you choose to be blind, you will not see.
Beliefs can move mountains even if considerable time must elapse for the invention of earthmovers.
We may deny our potential by not believing it, but we cannot deny that our desires to accomplish what has never
been accomplished must first proceed with a belief that our success is possible. Therefore our belief in
advancement or success becomes the cornerstone of victory.

Awaking the Discriminator

The scenario to follow describes a vicious street assault with you as an imagined victim. Such a crime could be taking place in any back alley in the world. As you read it, take note of the various levels of response acted out by the victim. At the end of the book we will revisit this scenario with a new set of eyes. I hope to show you how much more succinct the categories of the victim's defensive reactions appear.

The Assault

On the way to your car that night you didn't see them. Now your life is threatened. A shocking, skull-jarring blow from behind numbs your mind, buckles your legs, and releases a warm fluid that streams down your lacerated scalp. Despite a few seconds of momentary unconsciousness, your primitive reptilian brain senses hands forcefully trying to subdue your arms. It switches on your millions year old fight reflex. You twist instinctively with brute, impulsive strength. You tear one offending arm off but another tightens. The grip is simply too strong to break. One attacker holds you as another rains ruthless fists upon your face and head, each more violent than the previous. You jerk backward, barely avoiding a sharp object brushing your face. Your assailant has a knife! The sight jolts your adrenaline system giving you enough energy to break the clutch. Still a relentless onslaught of fleshy tentacles tries to subdue you. You barely escape one grab by circling your arm out of it. Wiping a sheet of blood from your face you count three shadowy forms. Thick-muscled arms lunge for your throat. You push back, hard. Outweighing the shadow, it tumbles backward. A second, bigger shadow tries the same tactic. You retreat at the moment of his lunge sending him stumbling forward. He did not expect to meet emptiness. For no conscious reason, when he gets up and lunges at you again, instead of pushing directly into him or stepping back, you slip your arms up under his, and lift him high onto his heels. You sense his confusion and surprise that he cannot budge you. Undeterred, the other two shadows continue their assault.

Eighteen seconds have elapsed since your head took its first concussive blow. With one attacker stalled your mind hits a clearing. A new resolve emerges. Survival instinct has fully kicked in from the rush of adrenaline into your bloodstream. Dilating blood vessels are pumping raw oxygenated energy into your limbs. You stonewall the next punch with your rising forearm, then surprise yourself by kicking instinctively into the shadow's groin. He drops, writhing in pain, clutching a ruptured testicle. As if a channel had suddenly switched in you head, the reality floods in that you are, and have been for thirty years, a martial *sensei*. That first traumatizing blow had blunted your skills from consciousness. Now, they spring back with a vengeance. Your trained response unleashes full force. You tuck your pelvis, coordinating the action with a deep and focused exhale. Your thumb springs on top of your rolled fingers and your legs widen to buttress your punch. The closest shadow never sees your piston-primed fist rocket forward. It slams into his sternum snapping his sternal notch from its cartiliginous hinge and slices into his viscera. The third shadow with the knife lunges in desperation.

Your moves gain fluidity as you drop into a *neko-dachi* cat, catch/*hiki-te*, and withdraw. Your breath floods into your primed, energy-filled dantien. Suddenly, your armed assailant experiences an immediate and pervasive body weakness from the 'suck/spit' energy technique your Okinawan sensei once taught you. Before he regains his stability you chop deep into his carotid artery, compressing it, causing a severe drop in his blood pressure. Disoriented and desperate to avoid falling, he grabs your arms. You seal his chest gates depriving his chi from entering his upper arms then easily lock onto his wrist and torque the knife from his fingers. He is at your mercy. Summoning chi into your eyes you assume the Tiger's Gaze, beckoning your attackers with your palms upward to enter your iron ring of power. Fear-striken, one assailant turns in retreat. He stumbles head long into three police officers.

The muggers are collared and charged with assault and battery against a civilian. The officers press you for details of the assault. You compassionately decline to press charges despite your deeply lacerated brow. You later lament that being a Buddhist and remembering to show compassion to all living beings is not an easy rule to practice. For weeks after the incident you meditate, sending compassion to the three assailants hoping that they find a clearer path for their future lives and that you find a safer path home from work.

Opening The Gates To Warrior Power
In the ideal dojo one's training would follow a prescribed developmental sequence analogous to an infant's physical progress from gross to fine motor skills. You crawl before you stand, stand before you walk, walk before you run. But many variables such as personal distractions, limitations of time, energy, intelligence or money etc., can impede progress causing a student to miss, overlook, or skip crucial training steps. Body size and/or physical temperament, degrees of perceptual or emotional maturity, intellectual capacity, or unexpected life events, can also cause a premature opening or closing of various energy gates in the mind/body complex. Big men engaged with smaller men often overlook the use of technical finesse. Smaller men tend to avoid direct confrontational tactics with larger men. Women and men have different emotional orientations to conflicts. Also, one's martial teacher may prefer one group of techniques or strategies over others, ushering their students into a skewed or narrow knowledge field, like teaching striking techniques but excluding grappling moves.

In my classes I have observed a natural ascendancy of powers in a generally logical progression through seven stages or "gates" of power. Skills in the first two to three gates are commonly taught and acquired in most dojos of the world. But it's rare for either a layman or a self-trained martial artist to pass through the latter four gates without expert guidance. In my opinion, these more obscure levels represent the real treasures of the Martial Ways.

Warrior Nature

Warrior nature is that part of every human's physical and psychic makeup activated whenever we must face serious challenges or threats. Everyone possesses a warrior nature. We feel it as a primitive and powerful physiology – a call of the wild. It is our warrior instinct that rouses us to freeze, flee, fight or, if you are exceptionally evolved, *flow*, in the face of danger. You do not have to be a member of an elite Martial Ways school to tap into this behavior. You don't need to own a karate gi, wear a black *obi*, or have a personal sensei to guide you in facing danger. We all have a built in, gut warrior instinct.

If you do seriously take up a martial art, expect your training to minimize your freeze/fright trigger and add tremendous skill and intelligence into your fight or flow mix.

Evidence of warrior nature is everywhere in modern society; a mother who instantly and automatically protects her child from an intruder; an untrained victim who furiously fights back in a street assault; a father who takes his son into the back yard to teach him how to protect himself; pacifists who 'fight' with an intense, non-physical commitment for their beliefs; athletes who 'fight' for the goal, point, or trophy. Sports are essentially ritualized mock combats. Some sporting events blur the line between real and mock conflict. Bullfighting is a kill-or-be-killed affair. Boxing, kickboxing, MMA (mixed martial art) matches represent modern day blood sports. Even dance, at its most primitive root, has been ascribed the festive recreation of the battle or the hunt.

Though we all have the capacity to tap into our warrior instincts, many of us do not possess more than a rudimentary grasp of the martial culture's rich layers of physical and psychological refinements to those instincts. This knowledge has been cultivated for centuries and across generations and cultures to protect and to expand us. Just because we do not consciously activate our warrior nature certainly does not deny its existence or relevance.

The Seven Gates Of Power

When I took up karate in the late 1960's I was fascinated by the art's awesome inventory of versatile hand and leg maneuvers. My eyes opened wide to joint locks and takedowns, submission holds, and pressure points. The list of ways to engage and vanquish my imaginary opponents seemed endless. In those early years I naively bundled all these techniques into the single definition of the Martial Ways as a great "physical" discipline.

Mind seemed of such puny importance next to my sinewy physique. It didn't seem that my gray matter mattered much at all. But as the years passed and my perceptions deepened, my opinion changed about karate's nature. What once seemed a vacuous entity, the concept of 'mind' or 'self', began to take on greater importance in my day-to day training. Decades later, I can honestly say that I was blind to the rich treasure of comprehensions that awaited me inside my mind/body/energy complex.

As a career teacher, I have had the great fortune of watching thousands of people over a forty year span explore their art - from their first awkward baby steps as *yakosei/hachikyu*, the blank slate beginner, to the mature and fluid power of the thirty-year senior. Because many of my students had crossed similar training milestones, I began to think of them as passing through a series of gates, gaining access to more elevated fields of experience and skill. Each new gate ushered them into new levels of personal power, meaning and value. I wondered if it was possible to catalog these gates or crossings by defining the exact powers they acquired and how they applied them. I didn't want to limit the concept of powers solely to the physical realm. Authentic power emerges not only through the living matrix of biological systems working in accord; the sensory, respiratory, musculo-skeletal, hormonal, neuronal, cerebral, etc., but the mysterious destinies of each practitioner as well. When all these systems, the visible and invisible, the Hard and the Soft, the known and the unknown, pull into accord, we can witness extraordinary powers unleash. I am not suggesting that wise men and woman can fly through the air. I mean 'extraordinary' in a heightened, everyday sense, as in 'extra' ordinary. For example, by slight adjustments to a physical technique, along with conscious attendance to the movement of interior energies, including one's mental state, anyone can affect a marked, even remarkable, increase in their physical strength that transcends our conventional ideas of power. These adjustments move one across a scale of crude to refined performance.

For my own teaching purposes I've earmarked seven primary gates or passages, seven phenomeno-logical events, seven transformative crossings for increasing physical power within a martial context.

The Seven Gates in Perspective

The *kanji* in the center of our school's logo above is called *chikara*—power. Japanese swordsmen distinguish two types: *tai chikara*, 'external' power, and *kokyu chikara* or 'internal' power. Both powers are ours for the taking. But we need to understand the source and nature of these types of powers if we wish to fully benefit from their flow. The seven-gate template to follow defines the primary strategies we use to engage our world—friend or foe. For the practicing martial artist, these seven strategic considerations make up a sliding scale of skill sets. These seven gates collectively represent the underlying platforms from which all martial technique can be evaluated. I consider them the underlying strategy of *all* human engagement.

Within each of the seven fields there are many specific techniques or methods that would be too daunting to present here. I simply want to provide a strategic framework around which all known martial techniques have developed. Many of you may readily identify familiar maneuvers in some of these fields.

I have also paired the three general state of consciousness previously discussed with each of the seven gates. Whether you practice martial arts or not, actions hot-wired into your DNA are often of the Common Mind state, i.e., commonly known or commonly practiced. Other actions will seem foreign, as they will require awakening unique or latent sensitivities. These will be paired with either the Uncommon or Quantum mindsets.

Functioning within the highest gates does not mean that the lower ones are less effective or should be discarded. That is not the intent of presenting this seven-gate template. Though these seven steps could be viewed as a graduating scale from gross skill resistance to more refined engagement, all the gates collectively represent a full spectrum of tools available to anyone for remedying the widest range of problems. One person's problem may require a flyswatter, another, a back kick, another, prayer.

Each level, each tool or gate presented, serves a particular purpose. Disputing that one way is the only way is merely the tantrum of a fragmented self. Kind words are not going to drive a nail into wood and a nail makes a poor action for resolving a career choice decision. Each gate therefore ushers us into a way to express our powers on appropriate levels of reality. The idea is to develop skill in each field and to gain competency with the entire toolbox of human potential. To learn how each tool/gate functions, how and for what situations each gate is best applied, and how we can negotiate our lives by using them effectively, gives us the best chance to survive and to flourish in the world. The main goal of holistic martial practice is wholesome and peaceful living.

THE SEVEN GATES OF POWER

☯ **Meditation** (Unifying the Triple Mind)

☯ **Direct Resistance** (Common Mind)

☯ **Yeilding To Gain** (Common Mind)

☯ **Complex Force** (Common Mind)

☯ **Physically Moving Internal Energy** (Uncommon Mind)

☯ **Mentally Moving Internal Energy** (Uncommon Mind)

☯ **Transcendental Tactics** (Quantum Mind)

GATE 1

MEDITATION

The Master Gate

Building Interiority – Awakening the Discriminator- Beckoning the Sacred Mind

'Rite makes authentic might'

As we engage the world with both eyes open and direct our deepest attention to the people, patterns, and things surrounding us, we enter the first gate of power—meditation. Be prepared. This gate will gush new information and energy. Meditation can open the floodgates of change that many in the West are still just beginning to grasp.

Just as the earth came into its power through the Big Bang of existence, we too can expand into our own unlimited power with the influential 'bang' of meditative connection. Meditation is our first gate of power. It galvanizes our interior energies, fosters insight, releases tensions, brings issues into focus, lowers blood pressure, stimulates endorphins, changes brain waves and increases physical strength. Meditation initiates the *seishindo*, the clear-minded path, in the hopes of later activating the *mushindo*, the transcendent or empty-mind path. One aim of meditation's inward journey is to clarify and to activate our own remarkable potencies.

Maturity can reveal that some skeptics are as unreasonable as the objects of their doubts. So it becomes an occasion for those who are wholly or partially blinded by their martial skepticisms to degrade the value of those who can see further and deeper. Therefore, just as it is helpful to be able to distinguish healthy martial practices from unhealthy ones, we must also learn to distinguish healthy skepticisms from unhealthy beliefs. We must challenge the notion that if we are blind to a part of our disciplines, then how blind? Or, if we can see, how clear is our vision? Otherwise, we can remain stuck in a limbo of *maybes*, which seldom get proven or disproven, but merely hold us to the *status quo*.

Meditation gives us an outlet for resolving some of our Life dilemmas. Remember, at their core, the martial arts were created to resolve conflicts. Its practice allows us to find, build, establish, and/ or reclaim fragmented inner ground. Every ounce of confidence gained is a piece of our power puzzle claimed. 'Being' is the most elemental definition of our human nature. Stripped of our social or self-imposed labels, such as warrior, mother, lover, employer, friend, judge etc., we simply are. Meditation grounds us into the source of our being. It draws us closer to our true face and conversely, to the source of our impasses. A notable family therapist once stated that he would rather be a human 'being' than a human 'doing.' If we are always doing, never pausing to reflect on our life actions, we can too easily loose sight of *why* we are doing them. I've watched thousands of martial students doing their arts in the dojo yet seldom witnessing their own authentic natures behind their actions.

Meditation is the act, the practice, and the art of grounding our daily doings into our daily being. Meditation irons out the wrinkles of self. It establishes an inner forum for mediating our discordances. It strengthens moral resolve and it directs us to that harmonious midline/balance between our inner and outer worlds.

Practically, for many, meditation is the simple act of sitting quietly. Meditation opens up a silent internal dialogue with parts of ourselves seeking healing, accord, power, resolve or integration

with other, alienated, oppositional parts of our character, those that pull us into isolation, discord, separation, ill-ease, thus dividing us into the *Other* Self, or what one precocious nine year old student labeled, 'The Dark Me'. Meditation is the foundation for spiritual sensitivity and mindfulness. Meditation is a sacred and silent act beckoning our third eye of insight and intuition to open wide.

The 'sitting' I refer to isn't just stilling, comforting or pleasuring our physical bodies. Meditation seats the mind, akin to attending a theater performance where, as part of an audience, we sit quietly and patiently to observe a show.

In meditation the mind is brought into a universal theater to observe the actions of our own personal world, not the external landscape immediately surrounding us, which impresses upon our senses, nor even the exclusive universe viewed by what we could call our "tenant mind" or tenant mentality, but an equally grand interior from which our mental nature springs. In a meditative state we note subtle communications taking place that may appear as vast, mysterious, and complex as those on the outside of our skin. When you tune into your own organic, sensory dialogs, as confusing or as garbled as they may at first seem, you build inroads into the nature of your inner reality. You construct what I call "interiority." Meditation reveals to us our innate intelligence out of a seemingly infinite cacophony of sensations, passing thoughts, imaginations, emotions, bodily pressures, inner sounds, will and desires. If our insight deepens sufficiently, we might come to realize that our matrix of self resonates precisely to, and interfaces seamlessly with, our external environment and its events.

If, at the beginning of your meditation, inner events seem a jumble, it's only because our chosen mental platform generally focuses on safety and pleasure in the material universe first, rarely on that 'soft' energy universe within us. Meditation merges inside and outside events. As strange as this may sound, outside events are really just as intimate as the inside ones. No two persons share the same relationship with them. Meditation awakens the symphony inside. It links our flesh and blood with the things and cycles of the earth, the sun and the moon. We are not just this planet's temporary residents. We are its full time 'resonance.'

How To Meditate

Two obvious questions should be asked, "How do I meditate?" and "Is there a meditative practice best suited for martial artists?"

Historically, we've seen a great value in seated meditation, particularly in the Samurai Era of Japan with the adoption of the austere, Zen Buddhist practice of *Zazen* (seated meditation). If, however, you come from a traditional kata school, I suggest you try moving meditation since martial arts are intense movement disciplines.

This is accomplished through Kata or Form work with a goal other than combative emphasis. When coupled with specific visualizations and rhythmic breathing patterns, kata, which appear to be solely of combative nature on the outside, can become a powerful and integrative inner practice.

Whether you are a martial artist or not, the fundamental mechanics of meditation are simple and yet, may feel oddly elusive because of this very simplicity. To effectively meditate, regardless of your discipline, just sit, stand, lie, or move mindfully and attentively. Just breathe. Just be. Don't pretend. Don't expect. Don't hold on to anything.

You don't go to the theater to fall asleep. You arrive to attend, to observe a show. Likewise, in meditation you must stay alert to a wholly unique and customized performance. Here you will witness a parade of energy and information designed specifically for your attention. This show will in-form, re-form, and re-balance you.

Just as the theater management provides comfortable atmosphere for its audience by dimming the lights, quieting the house noise and focusing its stage lights front and center, productive meditation practice benefits from dulling harsh sounds, shapes, temperatures, lights, and colors in the immediate environment. Next is to relax into your body. Relaxing is an integral part of meditation. When you relax into your body you change its physiology and, by extension, you affect your mind. Every meditator prepares differently. Some might take a hot shower, put on lose garb, workout, drink herbal tea, find a special location, or listen to soft music to still their restlessness. Find your own way to transition from action to stillness. Unwind yourself of immediate responsibilities. Trust your intuition. Spend a moment visualizing yourself completely at ease. You don't have to follow any rigid dogma to meditate. After all, who taught the first person to meditate? Don't judge yourself. Just be. A little trial and error is a healthy way to learn. Self-discovery awakens natural responsiveness, which we so often repress when we are told how to do things that we already intuitively know.

As your mental stage lights move front and center simply observe the movement of your own mind. The curtain will rise on a grand show within. What appears a cacophony of sensations will cohere and advance you toward authentic power. You may not be able to make much sense of all the emergent thoughts, images, sensations or emotions as they flow through you, but consistent practice will reveal the true nature and workings of your mind.

Most can expect certain events to occur during their meditative evolution. Mental agitations may at first increase then later subside. Chaotic inner events may take on more succinct meaning. Intuitive awareness will awaken. Inner movement will begin to make more sense. An emerging awareness will see a link between various interior events, like how breathing reflects mood, or emotions bind with beliefs. Your physical body will release tension. Warmth will spread. Impulses of hope, happiness, peace, self-affirmation and potential resolution will manifest. A sense of meaningful communication will replace nonsense in your mind. It may appear as if some other part of yourself is speaking coherently to you.

Simple questions will arise. What is sitting? What is being? What is breathing? Are their better ways to sit, stand, move, breathe or just be? Access to clear answers lie in your ability to separate your normal and conventional behaviors and ideas from your natural (unconditioned) behaviors. Normal is what you have been conditioned to be. Natural is what you were before any such conditioning.

Common Impediments To Meditation Practice

In the U.S. society we need to replace the 'c' in medicate with a 't' for meditate. Society is moving so fast and consumerism is so deeply rooted in our behaviors that our economic survival has become juxtaposed to anti-consumer acts like still meditation. The practice of constantly doing, constantly consuming may, at first, feel and appear antagonistic to meditation practice, but of course, is highly desired in a consumer society. Therefore one of the greatest impediments to effective meditation today is the idea of wasting time; that somehow quiet, still or inward-directed body practice is in effect, doing nothing useful. In truth, meditation is the art of doing 'useful nothing'.

If material consumption halts meditation, then spiritual consumption defines it. Meditating allows us to experience the sheer pleasure of doing nothing - *absolutely*. During meditation you are not buying or being sold. You are not being 'should' upon. You are walking into the sacred ground of the Absolute.

Imagine feeling so good that you desired nothing more than to simply sit with yourself. Animals have us beat. Creatures take joy in just being what they are.

I remember enjoying the simple act of breathing so much one day that I wanted to take the day off just to walk around and breathe! A meditator's ideal is to feel the seamless connection of Life. It is pure joy to simply be. And it's free! Meditation is a natural, human, creature comfort. But we are often our own worst enemies in getting somewhere with these practices. First time meditators find their minds switching off or shifting priorities in ways that quickly sabotage their practice. This can occur as a host of rather timely agitations and/or mental justifications for skipping it. The unfamiliar is a threat to the comfort of our Tenant mind, another way to look at the Ego. For the tenant is always afraid the owner (Source) may chose to move back in and evict our current identity. Most of us vigorously defend the status quo of our inner world. But the threat of eviction is an illusion. The tenant will not be dispossessed. The tenant will be absorbed into the Source.

Although Meditation appears to be a physically passive, and internally organizing event, most people do not realize that it will have an immediate effect upon your physical strength and begin to improve your overall health. This is just one small glimpse into meditation's profound effects upon the body.

GATE 2

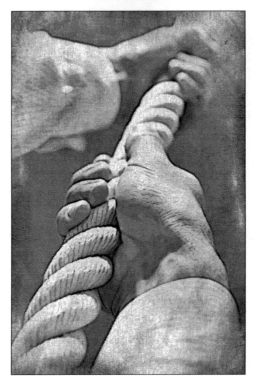

DIRECT RESISTANCE

Pull harder when pulled—Push harder when pushed

I remember being told, while witnessing my first karate board-breaking demo, that a successful break required, "mind over matter." I agree that the mind must overcome the body's natural resistance to strike the imposing solidity of wood or stone, but in fact, success requires mind *thru* matter. The concept of mind thru matter is one of the most elementary principles of martial arts technique. If you want to destroy matter you have to smash thru it, in our case, with our ever-handy, properly primed physical body.

Every child's first lesson about body power is that gross might takes the physical means away from any challenger who can't meet the same measure or standard of exchange. This fact is hardwired into us whether we are from Asia or Europe, the North Pole or the South, the victor or the victim. Only after the dawn of consciousness, around seven years old, do our innocent contemplations about worldly engagements get it into our heads that bigger, stronger, faster is how we win in life's gross arenas. This action tendency to meet force with direct, brute counterforce resides in our DNA. The things we encounter in the world seem best acted upon by moving directly and forcefully into them with straightforward and superior skill.

Obvious displays of hard body power are accomplished with gross musculo-skeletal skills. Superiority in these broad actions allows the strongest of us to conquer the less strong, the fastest to prevail over the slower, the able-balanced to withstand longer than the imbalanced, the smarter to rule the less organized, or the more enduring to outlast the less energetic. In the martial arena it becomes immediately obvious that to trump any challenger we must simply become better at the contest by one degree than our adversary. We just have to punch faster, kick harder, or block sooner. If the competition can lift one hundred pounds, we must lift one hundred and one. If she can run ten miles, we must run ten plus one step to secure victory. So the obvious hallmark of martial skill is our ability to outperform, outscore, out maneuver, out savvy our competitors in the ring, on the mat, or on the mean streets by matching our efforts eye for an eye, bead of sweat for bead of sweat, plus one.

Yet, we find ourselves possessing varying degrees of these broad talents. Some of us are quick but not strong, flexible, but lacking in power, more enduring, better balanced, or faster thinking. Some of our best skills are fleeting. They change as we age or adapt to new life circumstances.

Also, such strength differentials and fluctuations only become apparent during contests or conscious tasks. This is why so many cultures love competition. Contests define and refine us. They wake us up to what is actually achievable. They also cruelly point out our inequities, for in the Western competitive circuit we have created an imbalanced system where there is only room for one winner.

Thank god for two characteristics of our resilient lives; our bodies are capable of wily adaptation, and there exists teachers committed to showing us how to tap into and maximize our potential. With proper training, martial athletes have pushed themselves to extraordinary and victorious extremes.

The majority of martial routines press its student body to outperform their entry level abilities in seven primary skill categories: Strength, Speed, Endurance, Flexibility, Balance, Coordination, Re-

action time or Timing, Technical Diversity, and Perceptive ability. To secure victory in these arenas takes consistent and intelligent training.

This second gate of martial power is simple in principle. You will excel at the martial arts by enhancing all your biomechanical assets: the musculo-skeletal, circulatory, respiratory, hormonal and nervous systems. Orchestrating your body toward a greater standard of performance is the first step required for conquering the material world. In the gross physical arena 'might' rules over the less mighty. The maxim is 'expend the effort—extend the envelope.' Push your body to new heights of power. The primary tactic favored by all superior forces is direct confrontation.

GATE 3

YIELD TO GAIN

Push when pulled—pull when pushed

Have you ever witnessed a branch bend only to snap back with great stinging force? Have you ever gotten the sly notion during a tug-of-war that your victory might not lie in pulling harder but in briefly letting go, then pulling harder? Or did you ever consider that sidestepping a frontal assault might let your competitor fall face forward from his own force, saving you the task of taking him head on?

The 'gentle' arts of judo, tai chi, and aikido promote the tactics of pliability, yielding or blending as their first response to physical hostility. The American Dictionary defines *yielding* as means to give way to pressure, force or persuasion. Yielding has the peculiar quality of demasking aggression as a distorted behavior, for when you step aside, the aggressor falls from his own imbalance. Yielding could be called a 'first response.' What follows is the snap back.

The primary tactic favored by inferior forces is yielding. Yielding is considered the second gate of power because it often gets selected only when one lacks direct confrontational superiority.

The act of yielding however, is generally overlooked if one excels at direct confrontation skills and their adversary's haven't considered stepping aside. A 6'7", 320 pound man has little incentive to get out of anyone's way. Big persons—big in a broad way—not necessarily physical, seldom bend. Why should they? Big in most cultures equates to brute strength and sure victory. But in the martial arts we can see that some head-on forces can be skillfully manipulated to one's advantage by yielding. The art of Tai Chi Chuan has been noted for this central tactic, but it is available to all martial art systems.

ACTIVATING COMPLEX FORCES

Rise when pushed—Sink when pulled

Many forceful physical techniques directed against us can be cancelled with an action that avoids both direct confrontation or direct yielding. Instead, a specific and subtle angle of deflection—an oblique or tangential force—is applied that neither directly resists nor directly compliments the threatening force line. Many traditional martial blocks apply oblique force theory as the blocking action does not directly obstruct the opponent's attacking limb but rather, deflects it.

The beauty of this category of technique is that, in human-to-human engagements, it usually operates subliminally, that is, under the challenger's awareness. The opponent simply cannot figure out why his technique has been stymied. I've also seen many individuals effectively apply this specific tactic, themselves unaware of its principles.

Complex torque neutralizes outside forces by unconsciously shifting the adversary's actions into a counter-suppression, causing a mind/body schism. The opponent thinks his body is doing something that it is not. For example, I once watched a petite Russian woman ask a husky male football linebacker to hold a broom stick horizontally in both his hands then try to push her backward. She held the broomstick in the same fashion standing opposite to him. Despite outweighing her by at least 140 pounds, he couldn't budge her with his forward press. Remarkably, she held her ground with little strain.

She was successful because her complex torque misdirected his push, making him falsely think that he was pressing forward when his mind had switched his body's direction to resist her subtle rising motion by pushing downward. This principle is repeated millions of times throughout the world every day by every student executing a basic middle block. The puncher, when blocked, rather than continuing his punching force straight ahead, is subtly manipulated to push his arm sideways against the block. The sideways reaction neutralizes the punch's forward momentum, seriously reducing its impact, should it land.

Years ago I heard an interesting comment from a Buddhist martial arts master that the mind does not always know what the body is up to. To prove his point he told a willing subject that he would lightly strike his arm and within two days this person would piss blood. "Not to worry," he consoled his subject, "I've created a situation in which your mind mistakenly thinks your body had been injured in a way that it needs to purge itself of blood in order to rebalance itself." Truth be told, there was no physical injury. The subject's mind had been hijacked by a sophisticated technique that it did not understand. It initiated a physiological remedy that was not necessary. In a like manner, how many times have we blindsided ourselves with our own self-importance? This master affirmed that it's not that difficult to trick one's own mind or another's to go against itself.

Complex torque, though an uncommon action, is basically executed within the Common Mind framework. Once you understand the mechanics it's easy to apply.

Gates 2, 3 and 4 belong to and define the realm of the external masters. In my opinion 95% of today's world's martial arts community train exclusively within external principles. The three gates to follow usher one into the rarified realm of the internal masters.

PHYSICALLY MOVING QI

Stretch the front and contract the back when pushed
Contract the front and stretch the back when pulled

If Qi or Subtle Energy manipulation were commonplace I would not have to mention it to incoming students or to readers. However, in my decades of teaching, I've never enrolled a single beginner who firmly grasped this subject without prior training in an internal art. Many prospects hadn't given the subject any thought while a minority resisted the idea that any unseen energy actually existed.

Activating The 'Hard' Gates—Qi Over Li

Gates 2 through 4 focus primarily on what the Chinese call '*Li*' or external strength. The fifth gate of power begins the first of three stages of internal karate development. Stated earlier, the term 'internal energy' refers to Qi management or managing one's 'Energy Body.' After an astute sensei guides student's perceptions away from one-dimensional training frameworks, methods are implemented to heighten the sensitivities to actually feel Qi. The fifth gate awakens the Uncommon Mind to direct interior energies to increase physical strength, healing, and well-being.

At the earliest and most practical stages, under a teacher's guidance, internal energy is moved in a biomechanical fashion through musculo-skeletal manipulation. This type of energy activation is called *Hard Gate* manipulation. 'Hard' refers to hard matter—muscle and bone. Hard gates prime the overall body architecture for power through precise muscular acts such as moving limbs, rotating joints, assembling limbs relative to one another and/or the passing of limbs through various energy zones. All these motions and postures act as valves or levees to control Qi flow. The reason traditional karate kata are taught with such precision is due to the small margin of error before the Qi gets blocked or dissipated for a specific task.

MENTALLY MOVING QI

Activating the 'Soft' Gates
Intend Qi to the front when pushing—Intend Qi to the back when pulling

It is not necessary to physically move or touch another person (or objects) in order to affect them. History is rich with examples of energy transfers between individuals in the healing, meditative, and internal martial arts. This idea was once staunchly and skeptically disputed by Western science but more sensitive testing equipment continues to dissolve many of those doubts.

If the idea of affecting someone without touching them in a martial context is difficult to comprehend, consider two scientifically verified phenomena of how people and things are affected without physical contact.

The human heart emits electromagnetic signals that are conducted to every cell in our body. The heart's biomagnetic field emits signals 5,000 times stronger than our brain's. These signals have been proven to radiate outside the body and to affect the brainwaves of others in proximity. This phenomenon, called Cardioelectromagnetic communication, is influenced by intention and emotion.

Another phenomenon, called the Pauli Effect, reveals some people's ability to influence inanimate objects. The Pauli Effect was named after the famous theoretical Physicist, Wolfgang Ernst Pauli (1900-1958), a Nobel Prize winner in Physics. Pauli possessed a bizarre ability. He could cause experimental equipment to malfunction simply by being in its vicinity. Today the 'Pauli Effect' refers to the mysterious failure of technical equipment in the presence of certain people.

There are martial examples of non-touch phenomenon ranging across many eras, cultures, and martial styles. One example is the famous 19th century Japanese Samurai, Tesshu (1836-1888) founder of the *Itto Shoden Muto-ryu* school of swordsmanship. Tesshu was said to be so highly developed in his sword skills that some of his challengers conceded victory simply when encountering his intense gaze. Such is the power of internal energy. Tesshu's combat style was known as 'no-sword.' He believed that when a samurai realized there is no enemy, the purity of the style was all that was needed. Perhaps, Tesshu did not realize that such self-purification led to a super-organized energy body that electromagnetically disarmed his challengers. We can also see an example of Tesshu's internal tactics displayed in the Western boxing ring when one man tries to break his opponent's will with a stare down. What do you think is happening here?

Consider also, the foreboding psychological affects upon the ancient warriors who encountered the severed body parts of their comrades propped upon stakes. Such horror could demoralize one's opposition without ever 'physically' touching them.

The highest levels of combat actually initiate in our interior, in the organization and extension of our subtle energies.

The sixth gate ushers us across the threshold of legendary skills. To summon enough Qi that it can paralyze, immobilize, defuse, confuse or throw an assailant off balance or literally off his feet without the use of any physical action, where it is not necessary to contract one's muscles but enough to just forcefully intend!

Menscius, the 4th century Chinese philosopher stated, "Where the mind goes, Qi flows." And in the Taiji Classic, *Song of the Circulation of the Primordial Qi*, it is stated, "The mind (*Yi*) and Qi are rulers...Ruler and follower work together; Above and Below act in Harmony, and the whole body is one flow of Qi." When developed properly, this silent and invisible vitalizing wind will uproot even the most skeptical mind.

Our brain runs the current of our will power. Mental Qi is the mind's Subtle Energy reservoir. A strong will is equated to having strong energy. We use the term 'Soft Gates' to describe mental actions that distribute internal energy such as self-affirmations or negations, and other directives we give to ourselves. Intention distributes the willpower that drives our physical actions. Intention has two primary aims, to stimulate thought and to add cohesive power to the physical body. Coupled with specific breathing patterns, intention moves Qi through the bodily channels. It's often said, "Where there is a will there is a way," because a willful person is often one who gets his way. Kempo masters noted that shifting one's mental focus also resulted in an instantaneous shift in one's physical energy, because every mental event has its counterpart in the physical realm, and vice versa. That is, your Qi will flow to any body part your mind sends it to. And so, in the performance of traditional kata (form), it is understood that there is an *inner* kata (mind/energy pattern) that must accompany the outer body pattern. In the Japanese martial arts when these two foci, the physical and mental, are aligned, one is said to have *kime*. Kime is the alliance of a mind/body unwaveringly focused on one goal.

By contrast, Hard style actions tend to rely mainly on gross conditioned responses—a mix of instinct and habit. Gross-trained reflex can result in a semiconscious extension of energy into the body. I use the term 'semiconscious' because subtle disorganizations of the mind and/or body, unknown or unfelt by the transmitter, can dissipate the full force of a move. Internal training addresses these misalignments. Any sensei can tell you that most novice students expend huge amounts of energy with poor initial results when learning a new technique.

With the correct intention and proper focus on the body's refined energy systems we can dramatically increase our physical strength. The mind directs Qi to wherever our mental focus comes to rest. Qi instantly charges any part of the body it flows to acting like a covert cavalry reinforcement taking up its station alongside the regular battled-hardened trooper—our body.

TRANSCENDENTAL TACTICS

Direct loving, compassionate spirit to all push or pull oppositions

The seventh gate uses Transcendental Tactics to resolve conflicts. By transcendental tactics I mean the act of consciously altering, transmitting or receiving specific energy frequencies. Few students of the Martial Ways will ever penetrate, let alone, master this level of skill because the mind must be both highly receptive to finer flows of energy and accept the reality that everything is interconnected and in continuous, present, and influential communication via an invisible, vibratory network. Remember, you need to be Right brain aware.

Sages and scientists both tell us that all matter is vibrating energy and they agree that our supposedly 'solid' world is, in reality, mostly empty space with particles whirling about at different frequencies creating unique matter structures, including the human form. Scientists have not only measured the body's vibrational frequency while in various physical and emotional states but they have demonstrated that our mental states directly strengthen or weaken us. Internal martial artists learn to control their mind/body's vibrational fields to nullify and dissipate a wide range of problems. By using Transcendental Tactics to control our vibration rate we can eradicate many conflicts. Healing and empowering frequencies can be summoned with the proper guidance and training.

Meditation, the first gate of Power, sets this goal into action. Meditation plants the seed for our self-awareness to expand. Gates two thru six cultivate that seed. The seventh gate brings the seed to flower by letting our Quantum Mind tap into our wisdom's well.

For centuries martial arts have given us endless ways to vanquish our opponents. We pummel them with piston-like limb actions, twist their joints with calculated pressures, torque our punches from thick-muscled torsos; slap, pinch, rub, smack pressure points, or choke them out of their minds with well-placed forearms. Yet, few schools counter-balance these violent actualized, imagined or real thoughts and simulated actions with loving and compassionate feelings towards others, nor extend true care toward the planet as a whole to dissolve or defuse its toxic vibrations of negativity, manifested through its maligned channels of hatred, greed, and anger. Compassion is too often the unwelcome guest in the combative disciplines. By 'spiritual body' I mean the use of our whole being tuned to our higher and compassionate self, directing positive energies toward ending conflicts in the most peaceful manner possible. The highest form of martial expression is the transcendence of negative projections in all forms from the most base/physical conflicts to the finer strata of mental/internal discordances. Whenever we rehearse actions on the subtle, invisible, quantum or spirit level, we refer to them as 'spiritual' practices. These practices were designed to counterbalance the projections of aggressive physical training and negative thinking. The art of maiming, injuring, incapacitating or killing was to be equalized by the healing or making-whole arts. Otherwise, it was noted that the very imbalance of a dualistic perspective would perpetuate continual unrest in the quantum field. The masters understood that meditative introspection counterbalanced visceral release for balance to be restored and peace to reign. For the rare few, every fiber of their being becomes a beacon of health, peace and truth.

INTERNAL KARATE

Meditation began our journey into personal power. The seventh gate of Transcendental Tactics completes a full circle as we strive for a spontaneous, unconditional, and compassionate state of 'no conflict'. The task of the seventh stage is to extinguish the flames of core conflict within the self and to extend our compassion to all things. Transcendental Tactics enable us to transform the need for getting even, getting richer than, better than, or getting on top of, into getting balanced, sharing wealth, sharing health, and sharing the view. 'Get' is replaced with 'give'. In the end, the highest form of martial practice is not taking life or limb but granting life by giving evenness, giving balance, giving abundance, and giving health.

Healthy competition and practice, martial or otherwise, enriches all parties because it leaves no corruptive wake. The vanquished are not left behind, broken or berated. Everyone gets uplifted. The wisdom masters remind us that what we do unto others we do unto ourselves. If we are all linked, than vanquishing is a form of being vanquished. Modern physics affirms this indisputable proof in the underlining principle that for every action there is equal and opposite reaction. Here the concept of 'opposite' means that the ripples of any action will always return back upon its transmitter.

The seventh level of engagement activates the spiritual sensitivities to rise above our conflicts without resorting to violent physical engagement. And if one's destiny should fall into a vortex of unavoidable, hostile battles, we will have the basic skills in place to do what needs to be done.

PART 4
THE ENERGY BODY

"The day science begins to study non-physical phenomena, it will make more progress in one decade than in all the previous centuries of its existence."

Nikola Tesla

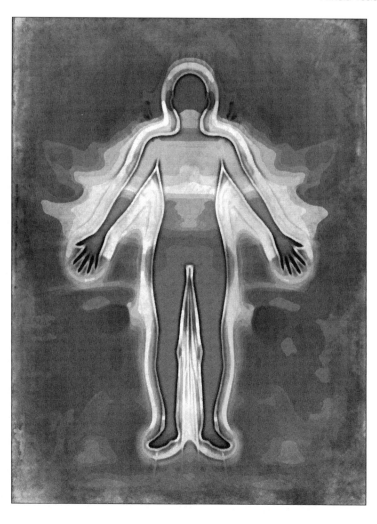

You Have An Energy Body

The single most important concept in this book is that *you* have an Energy Body. You were born into this world a twin. One part of you is visible. It is your flesh and blood, bone and muscle form. It's the part readily seen and touched and the one with which you have the most familiar working relationship.

Your companion form is invisible. It has an ethereal nature. It consists of a bio-field of high frequency energy waves, expanding and contracting, growing or diminishing, aiding or retarding, *all* your physical actions. It functions like a genie in your body-bottle working behind the physical scenery to rescue you at the drop of a clear intention. It is the hidden alchemist behind the *Mystery of Power* stories at the beginning of this book.

The ancient masters recognized this formless form and, over time, they sought four primary objectives with it: Awaken to its flow—Gather it—Cultivate it—Advance its practical/combative, therapeutic/medical, and spiritual/meditative goals.

The brutish attack with raw physical strength.
The warrior defeats his enemy with superior technique.
The better-trained defeat the lesser-trained.
The metaphysical warrior defuses the energy that leads to the conflict,
The Buddha flows where there is neither defeat nor non-defeat.

How Internal Martial Arts Came To Be
A Condensed History Of The Birth Of Internal Karate

Let's look at one hypothetical overview of how our Energy Body might have been discovered and its movement principles codified by masters past.

Archeological and anthropological records tell us that we evolved from pre-human, apish creatures, barely separable from the foraging animal world. The earliest primal men were instinctive and animalistic. They suffered no separation anxiety of mind from body or head from heart. They had no high functioning cerebral neocortex (forebrain) and probably little, self-evaluating consciousness. It is doubtful that primitive man had the ability to pause for reflection, that is, think deeply about his own thoughts. As a mostly stimulus/response-based creature his rudimentary self-conscious left him bereft of complex conceptual strategy.

However, our primal ancestors had direct access to their animal powers and instincts which allowed them to fight with savage determination and impressive power-to-weight performance.

The modern Neo-cortical man that followed was radically different. He thought, evaluated, reflected. He planned, then he executed. He could hold and weigh both past and present in his mind's eye. As the human stimulus/response equation grew more intricate our brain's neuroplasticity followed suit leading to the development of an increasingly more complex neural structure. Environmental and mental changes walked us hand-in-hand into an ever-complicated future.

Civilizing the animal in man (i.e., making the beast civil) has caused us to tradeoff some important grounding instincts. Instead of relying solely on bodily skills for survival, we began to favor tool usage. Tools, as an efficient body extension, activated new mental strategies tipping the scales further in favor of more cognitive involvement. From the civilizing perspective we needed to advance our tools and technologies to meet the demands of a growing and complex society, but from a martial perspective, a mind/body schism began. As we became more cerebral, placing greater trust and emphasis in the use of our minds, we began to over-rely on 'thinking it thru' over 'gutting it out.' We are now losing our once acute sense of body touch with the organic world, replacing it instead with an acute sense of 'techno-touch' in our expanding technologic world. Greater numbers of people are shedding their animal instincts and powers in exchange for the heightened mental powers to gain mastery over our technological tools. Technology is our new gut. We let the SUV, the calculator, or the Internet's Google Search *muscle it out*. All well and good on one level. Without question, these are efficient methods for getting things done. But technology is eroding the subtle body wisdoms that our physical natures possess. We are becoming desensitized to our physical body world.

Environmental hostilities have not ceased as a result of modernizing social structures, laws, and technologies. Human-to-human violence continues unabated throughout the world since our earliest ancestors walked the earth. No end to our aggressive behaviors appears in sight. *Man*power is still

called for on many occasions. We know that some ancients attempted a synthesis of primal strengths with cognitive evolution to enhance their overall prowess. Some Chinese masters studied and mimicked other creature powers. Perhaps, they discovered that they had not really lost their *primal force* but had let it atrophy. As our modern minds have grown in both prominence and self-importance, our bodies have simultaneously diminished in value. We could make a crude analogy that white-collar (cerebral man) sees himself as a transcendent entity to blue-collar (primal man). When a will turns predominantly toward mental abilities it reduces its physical nature. This causes a head/rich, body/poor syndrome. From what I have witnessed, our civil mind has, by degrees, abandoned those sensitivities that once intimately connected us to our Subtle Body energies. Having firmly ensconced our egos in the White Tower of our skulls we now find ourselves less grounded as a culture to the organic world surrounding us, including awareness of the perplexities of our own insides. Nowhere is this more evident then in the younger generation, plagued by obesity, Attention Deficit, Hyper Active issues, entertainment addictions, and a noticeable loss of sharp physical reflexes. Any professional martial artist who has been teaching children over the last three decades has seen a dramatic and disturbing drop in children's body awareness and physical skills.

Perhaps, intuiting that something vital needed preserving or reawakening, astute seekers in the past began to re-evaluate their physical nature and reawaken their latent animal-energy currents. These inquisitives found that they could tap their own wildness and dramatically increase their physical strengths and perhaps, even restore an aspect of animal greatness alongside their cognitive evolution. Such practices became the lost keys to a primitive power ignition with a unique upside. Modern man could do something that primitive men and the animals could not. Our enlarged brain capacity could study these powerful currents and advance them. This codification process has been going on in the martial arts for thousands of years. The martial arts became the perfect place for the synthesis of an animal-wise and spiritual-wise Life warrior.

Understanding Your Subtle Energy Body

The Subtle Energy Body consists of multi-layered vibrational energy fields circulating in and around us in specific channels at specific frequencies. These energy fields compliment our hard matter constitution of organs, bone, muscle, fluids, nerves, hormones etc. (themselves energy fields of tightly bonded molecules). The subtle fields are comprised of electro-magnetic, light, sound, photonic and chemical forces. They are regulated by a complex cosmic/earth/mind/body synergy. The Chinese named some of the unseen channels, meridians, which were meticulously mapped by Chinese doctors in their 3,000 year-old science of acupuncture. Like miniature rivers, these channels have two main currents or polarities—positive (Yang) and negative (Yin), each with sub-branches. Most acupuncture books highlight the meridians and their specific acupoints.

My study of the Subtle Energy Body began one year after attending a pressure point seminar given by a prominent East coast Karate master. Rather than learning the points themselves, I became curious about their underlying principles. I had lots of questions; Why do pressure point strikes work? Was everyone affected equally? If not, why not? What is the relationship of a pressure point to a meridian? Can meridian flow be controlled or altered? How fast does Qi flow in a meridian? What makes it flow? Do all meridians flow the same? What affects these currents? How do we know if we are affecting these flows? What role does the mind play in moving Subtle Energy? Is the mind Qi? Is Qi consciousness? Why do certain meridians flow up the body while others flow down? Is the flow consistent? How did this flow get started? Can it be measured in volume, valence or voltage? Can Qi flow be increased? How? How would we know if we had an obstruction in a meridian and how would we know if we had removed an obstruction? Can one have too much or too little Qi? What are the consequences of too much or too little energy for martial artists? How can this knowledge make me a better more efficient marital artist and a better, healthier human being?

Energy Work In Martial Training

Internal or Subtle Energy work *was* and *is* part of many Asian classical and traditional martial arts. This component was and is recognized as a means of maintaining vitality, enhancing mental clarity, and infusing extraordinary strength into any martial technique. We are at a point in martial history where our accessibility to these principles has never been closer at hand. All we need now is the motivation to grab them.

The Physics Of Training

The fundamental forces in the universe are not just exerted upon us. We too are the living physics of the earth. We receive and exert these forces back upon the world. All the world partakes of a

great give-and-take cycle. There are four known fundamental forces in nature. They play a central role in making our universe what it is today. Three of these forces operate at near similar strength. One, called the Strong Force, binds the atoms of the nucleus together. Another, called the Weak Force, is responsible for nuclear decay; the third, Electromagnetism, which is of particular interest to internal martial study, not only holds electrons in their orbits, but causes electric and magnetic effects (attractive or repulsive) between any piece of matter carrying an electrical charge—including *us*! Lastly, there is Gravity which, we know all too well in the martial arts, contributes to the control and manipulation of balance and weight, a critical component of physical conflicts. The important point is that the properties of these four forces reside within all of us.

Outside of the obvious physics of moving our physical mass at a higher speed to generate impacting power, it is of particular interest the we can also generate an electromagnetic, auric or etheric field, which exhibits both linear (electric) and spiraling (magnetic) properties. This subtle field generates an invisible force like an Xray that can both penetrate and alter other energy fields.

These forces, these streams of Subtle Energy, fuel our brain, muscles, and bodily organs. They boost our actions, light up our biological systems and enhance the structures they flow through like water coursing through a turbine. If a current cannot reach a muscle, that muscle will lack the 'juice' for full contraction. It has been known for centuries that breath is one of the prime regulators of these currents. Breath is our bridge to controlling some of these fundamental forces. For example, in the internal martial systems various types of breath control are used to alter the respiratory process to affect both the directionality and intensity of our electromagnetic field flow. Exhalation versus inhalation, chest breathing versus belly breathing, extended breaths versus short breaths, silent versus audible breaths, all create various inner push/pull motions that alter energy flow in the body to effect, not only our physical strength, but the physical strength of those in immediate proximity to us.

The world is engaged in a great conflagration and we are some of its prime players. The four fundamental forces are pillars supporting the stage for this grand show. All our action scripts follow the principles of physics. Internal martial arts give them a dynamic interpretation.

We are the living physics of the earth
The micro-reflects the macro

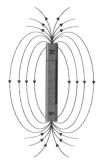

The magnetic field of an electromagnet (EMF)

Earth EMF

Human EMF

INTERNAL KARATE

Energy Flow Chart

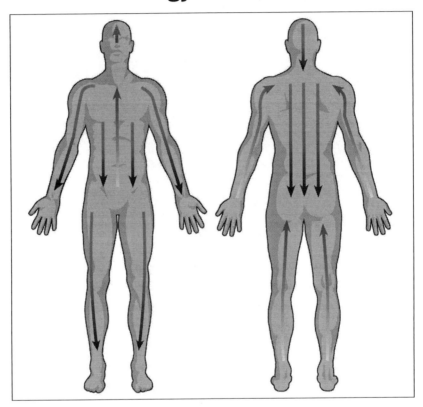

This illustration depicts the body's major surface energy channels and their direction of flow. It's not necessary to memorize specific meridians. Just get a general sense of the energy movement indicated by the arrows. You can activate this chart kinesthetically, by rubbing your hands along your body surface in the direction of the channel flow. Rub your entire body from top to bottom. Build a kinesthetic memory of the direction of flow. This simple exercise will help you to move QI along its pathways and remove subtle obstructions or blockages. Doing this energy massage a few minutes a day, or as part of your martial warm up will increase your physical strength, health, and well-being.

Before starting any energy work take a moment to 'go inside' and scan your body. The simple act of noticing your mood, feelings, and sensations will gather energy inside your body. You may experience a wide range of internal shifts depending upon your level of sensitivity just by switching your mental focus away from your outside world to your inside one.

Two Qi Drivers

Qi is propelled in and around your body by means of two drivers. One is respiration. Deep belly or abdominal breathing is the most effective way to distribute a healthy volume of Qi throughout your trunk and limbs. The other driver is mental intention. The mind drives Qi through the cognitive act of *willing*, and with certain overrides to the mechanical engine, via voluntary respiration. Will or mental Qi fuels our intention. Intention drives Qi through our body. Conversely, respiration drives Qi through the mind. Our biological systems are in a constant recharging and rejuvenating cycle where the body pumps/pushes/fuels the mind and the mind pumps/pushes/fuels the body.

Getting A Grip On The Subtle

Newcomers into internal energy practices are often excited but bewildered about how their Subtle Energy system functions beyond cellular metabolism, which converts chemical energy to mechanical energy. I pose this initial question to get them started. "Does clenching your fingers into a fist cause energy to flow into or out of your hand?" Many karate students are initially stumped. If you answer that energy flows into your hand, then shouldn't it follow that you could clench your fingers indefinitely? Yet, we know intuitively that this cannot be true. The finger muscles eventually fatigue, and as they do, the tension diminishes.

We can logically deduce that energy must be flowing out of the hand. Eventually your finger muscles tire because you will have depleted your muscle's energy reserve.

An important and basic principle of energy flow is demonstrated in this action. My question rightly perplexes beginners because the way I asked it is actually faulty. I purposely biased the question to only half of the real energy equation. Clenching the fist does not result in an either/or effect. Muscular tension expends energy for contracting the fingers, but only for half of its musculature. Energy also simultaneously fills the finger muscles for extension.

Recall one of the most basic laws of physics, Newton's Third Law of Motion; *"for every action there*

is an equal and opposite reaction." That means that two events take place simultaneously. Applying this principle reveals two critical actions surrounding finger muscle activation. While the flexors contract the digits, the extensors stretch them. These two complimentary actions create a balanced formula for all physical actions.

I consider this one of the most essential observations the ancients made about the nature of the body's Subtle Energy system. However, this cornerstone insight was just the beginning. More profound revelations were to follow. You cannot cultivate what you are not aware of. You cannot properly use an energy or tool you do not understand, cannot feel, or do not believe exists. Awareness must precede correct manipulation. Awakening these sensitivities takes practice. The clear mind must precede the empty mind. One must remain, in all cases, mindful.

To continue, if energy goes out of the fingers by contracting them, then how do we get energy to reopen our hand? A simultaneous counterbalancing event must occur. As the energy releases from the contracted musculature of the fist, the brain/body directs energy to refuel the stretched musculature. Stretched muscle draws Qi into it. Even lightly elongating a muscle will charge its fibers similar to the way a drawn bowstring builds up kinetic energy for the arrow's release. This energy-shifting process follows a precise course. *As contracted muscle discharges—stretched muscle charges.* It's a brilliant system. Why do you think the world's martial artists practice so often with their fists chambered at their hips before they punch? Chambering stretches the deltoids for maximum acceleration of the arm—a direct result from the energy inflow prior to its release.

I believe that after observing this reaction the early masters asked this follow up question, "Will a physical motion be stronger if its primary musculature is pre-stretched? Their discovery—absolutely!

This historic leap of logic gave birth to centuries of brilliant internal manipulations. A second crucial question shaped the internal arts mechanical foundation; "Is it possible to borrow, redirect, transfer, transmit or carry the charge from one muscle group to enhance another? This intuition proved correct again. It was discovered, for example, that a person could draw energy from the right side of their body into their left side. Suddenly a huge set of possibilities arose and along with that, the complex study of all the different charging and discharging actions that could take place by various changes in posture between muscular contraction and stretch. Stretching proved a powerful activator of internal energy currents. Stretching aligns the muscle fibers for better firing. It advances Qi into the muscles to increase their charge. A contracted muscle discharges energy. Conversely, a stretched muscle draws energy from its elongation. It's a great give and take orchestration. As we give, so we take. As we give out energy, so we take in energy. This is the organic foundation of the philosophical principle, *"give and you shall receive."*

It was also discovered that the auric field surrounding the body could manipulate another's auric field, strengthening or weakening it. When the martial monastics got hold of this knowledge they took these internal principles into the frontier of the mind to accomplish feats of which the Western world is just now comprehending. These early, logical leaps birthed today's high end martial practices. How do we know past martial masters knew this? They left their principles embedded in their kinesthetic treatises called *kata*. Every principle I have discussed in this book can be found in the essential kata patterns from Asia.

Within many older martial systems the elaborate corridor into internal principles took place through the study of the traditional forms. It's one thing to think about, reflect, or contemplate the subject of internal power. It's altogether different to consciously attune to and move your own energy field. *"Repetition is the key to power."*

The energy corridor that opened for me took place with isshinryu's Sanchin kata. Unfortunately, many attempts by Western teachers to define this particular kata's esoteric nature have been far too shallow which has lead thousands of students (including myself) astray for years with superficial, mainstream interpretations (like 'vein popping', the simple tightening of the body for the sole purpose of tensing) creating more confusion than clarity about this pattern's vital purpose.

Esoteric Sanchin was designed to move internal energy. Sanchin's best kept secret, even today hidden from many professionals, is that it was created to emphasize and exercise the *Energy Body*, not just the physical body. The Ancient Chinese provide us, within its structure, a template called the Five Element Theory for understanding how five distinct internal energy orientations, or what we refer to as 'attitudes' could be cultivated and controlled.

Early Chinese philosophers linked five primary and interdependent life functions that defined the actions of humans, earth, and the universe. They gave these five phases simple labels: fire, earth, metal, water and wood. Each element had many corresponding relationships with one another. One relationship, appropriate for martial purposes, is directionality. That is, each element could represent a direction; Fire = upward motion, Earth = rotational or circular motion, Metal = contracting or retracting motion, Water = descendant or lowering motion, and Wood = expanding or outward mo-

tion. The Five Element template clarifies one of the base levels of physical forms practice. According to this theory, any limb action must move in one of the five elemental directions. The Sanchin kata teaches one how to direct inner energy flow through a process we call **gating**, (specific muscular contractions, breath work and mental visualizations) to direct Subtle Energy into the primary musculature needing activation. If you want to punch harder, a Wood element motion, Sanchin teaches you the proper biomechanics to funnel the maximum Qi into your punching limb.

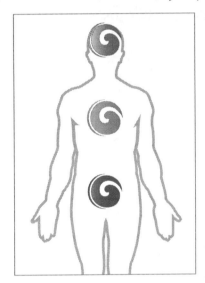

Why The Lower Dantien Is The Seat Of Martial Power

Our bodies have three significant energy reservoirs that are activated with the proper focus. These three reservoirs are called *dantiens* in China, (*tandens* or *ki hai* in Japanese). The word means 'Field of Elixir' or 'Sea of Chi.' They are often described simply as the upper, middle, and lower dantiens. The upper dantien is centered between the eyes. It is sometimes referred to as the 'third eye,' for its ability to see/sense energy. This dantien is the reservoir of psychic or mental energy and its productive output is **knowledge/intuition.** The middle dantien is located in the heart region in the center of the chest. Its productive output is **wisdom** or **heart knowledge.** The lower dantien or Cinnebar (red frequency) field is the one we will concentrate upon in this book. Its productive output is **physical power** (*chikara* as mentioned earlier). The lower dantien is considered the seat of martial power

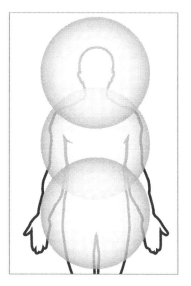

for this reason. It activates the body's muscular engine. This dantien encompasses an area within the lower body core located just beneath the navel. Qi naturally accumulates here like a reservoir contains a river. When you fill your belly tub, your meridians, like rivers, rise. Full rivers lead to a body filled with vitality and thus full-strength actions. However, in order to gather bodily vigor you must meet some fundamental criteria: you *must* relax, center yourself into your body and maintain a straight and aligned spine. One of the simplest ways to center into your body is to belly breath, to draw your breath into the lowest part of your lungs which causes the abdomen to swell. Belly or abdominal breathing roots the mind into its physical nature. As martial artists, we don't want to be head rich and body poor during physical activities. This is the primary reason that old world teachers shunned talk or too many questions from their students. It's not that questions are inherently bad, but too much thinking and talking during practice shifts vital energy away from the limbs. The immediate value was placed upon *doing* rather than *thinking about the doing*. The proper place for thinking about doing lies mostly in the preparation for physical activity, not in the execution of the activity itself. Here the mind's primary task is to hold concentration on the required body skills.

To get a better understanding of how the three dantiens function, imagine each of them as separate, colored spheres encompassing roughly one third of your body. The upper dantien envelopes not

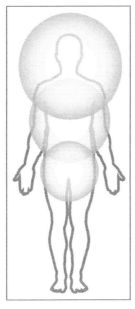 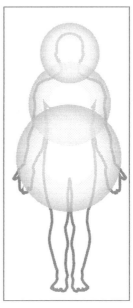

**Western Culture's Energy
Orientation**   **The Martial Ideal**

only your head, throat and upper chest, but extends outward a foot or so around your body. Imagine a large bubble encompassing the top third of you. The middle dantien represents a second bubble enveloping your chest. The third or lower dantien encircles your waist and hips. These dantiens over-lap. They communicate. They radiate energy. They cause shifts in mental, respiratory, neural and endocrine function. The most significant observation made by the early kempo pioneers in regard to the dantiens was their ability to expand and contract both voluntarily and involuntarily. This means that each person has an opportunity to control his own energies to optimize success in any particular endeavor.

When a task is called for, the energy of the spheres shifts to that part which is most needed. A *physical* task requires that we distribute energy into the lower dantien, which fills the belly with Qi, enhancing torso and limb strength. A *mental* task distributes energy to the upper portion of the body to increase our concentration powers. When a strong mental focus is required we often still the body to draw from the lower dantien's reserves. When our emotions are engaged, energy is drawn into our chest. The heart chakra, our feeling center, is activated. Energy concentrates in the upper torso. During these natural transitions we never completely dissolve any one sphere when drawing energy from another. This can be likened to the way in which we never completely empty out our lungs on exhalation. A residual amount of air always remains. This is also true in regard to dantien functioning. If you are sensitive enough, you will feel the three dantiens shifting as your world engages you on the mental, emotional, and physical energy planes. You will not feel a line of demarcation dividing one sphere from the other but you should feel a graduated tidal flow as your energy moves up and down your body.

Many years ago I came across a small martial arts manual that pointed out how the Asian masters felt that a pear shaped body was the ideal martial form. The pear shape gave a person a low-rooted energy center. A large belly was indicative of great vitality, a vast sea of Qi. I was disappointed reading this because I realized that my lithe, thin frame would never be bell shaped. It wasn't until twenty years later, when I took up internal study, that I realized the image the Asians were talking about was not the shape of one's actual physical body but the shape of one's Energy Body!

The internal flow of Qi, one of many bodily rhythms, occurs naturally and effortlessly, but not always efficiently. Concentrated training can dramatically improve the manner in which this energy aids us. For example, nearly everyone will fight if seriously threatened. The will to survive releases a torrent of survival energy. But any sensei can tell you that untrained people, whether they win or loose, are mostly disorganized fighters.

In Buddhist Kempo we learn to open, cultivate, and balance these three energy spheres or centers. We study the mechanisms that cause these fields to shift. We learn to 'oil the energy hinges' so to speak, to reduce frictions during energy distribution from one sphere to another and to dissolve dysfunctional fixations that might impede its movement. When forms such as the Okinawan Sanchin kata are practiced with the correct understanding, students can accomplish a free flowing energy system. Internal martial arts such as *Tai chi*, *Hsing I* and *Bagua* focus heavily upon unrestricted energy flow. Sadly, much of this inner legacy has been disappearing as the arts have spread from Asia into Western cultures. The madcap and exciting pace of modern life has turned many young minds away from the richness and depth of the body's wisdom found in the practice of the authentic martial disciplines.

Empty Standing

Early Chinese philosophers believed that before the universe formed, a primal emptiness, an infinite nothingness, called *Wuji* or *Wuchi* existed. *Wu* means 'negation.' *Ji* means 'beginning'. Some thought it might be possible to recreate this empty state within the body/mind complex to recapture a source power. They devised a simple standing exercise that has become one of the oldest energy cultivating practices developed in Asia. They named it *Wuji,* or *Jan Jung,* 'Standing Strong' or 'Standing Like a Tree'. We call it *Empty Standing*. Unlike the Western ideal that intense physical activity is necessary to derive any meaningful body benefit, Empty Standing strives for an internally dynamic action in an otherwise still body. In Japanese, Korean, and Okinawan kata there is an instance of Empty Standing in the initial salutary postures prior to commencing and concluding these ritual forms.

The Western world is a restless, driven civilization. Our restlessness appears as stress in the form of constriction, tension, nervousness, anxiety, and subtle pathologies that degrade our biological systems and block Qi flow. Empty Standing counters stress by aligning our head, spine, and pelvis to reduce the body's mechanical pressures thus creating a true and centered self-equilibrium. The postural alignment and relaxed musculature that results from the consistent practice of Empty Standing keeps Qi channels open, which invites us into a more profound state of relaxation and, in turn, unlocks deeper energy resources. Empty Standing also focuses the mind inward engaging our intuition to further release additional physical and mental stressors. This simple exercise can open and clear the body's energy channels and reduce, halt, or eliminate developing disease states. Mental stress is a world pandemic eating at us from the minute we awake. *Empty Standing* is perfect for quieting and easing distracting mental chatter. A calmed mind adapts quickly to circumstances and thinks with greater clarity.

Activating Your Energy Body

Empty Standing is an easy 'body meditation' practice. Begin by standing with your feet straight, shoulder width apart and knees slightly bent. Relax and let go of your daily concerns. Let tensions melt away. Center your weight over the point that lies just above your foot's arch where a slight hollow appears in the front center of the ball. This is called the 'Bubbling Springs' acupuncture point. Next,

---

Eight Step Mind/Body Rejuvenator

Practice any step below for 3 minutes individually or in the sequence indicated.

Empty Stand without any other mental agenda.

Scan and relax your body. Let go of all tension from head to toe.

Focus on your breath. Don't control it, just attend to your breathing.

Breathe into your lower abdomen (dantien).

Guide your Qi in the Small Circle Orbit for 3 minutes or 9 cycles (see page 139).

Sync your breath with your conscious Small Circle Orbit and

 the six undulatory movements in the sequence described above.

Sync up your conscious guide and breath along with the six undulations.

imagine the center of your head suspended from a string attached to the 'Hundred Meetings' acupuncture point. Gently "tuck and suck," as one master stated. That is, tuck your pelvis forward and suck in your abdomen. Lift your elbows a few inches from your side so that your hands rest near the top of your thighs. Gaze softly into the distance. Lightly place the tip of your tongue at the roof of the mouth. The tongue naturally adheres in this position for most people. Exhale slowly, allowing your abdomen to contract slightly. When inhaling, simply allow the lungs to effortlessly draw in energy.

Practice Empty Standing at any time. Early morning and outdoors is optimal when the air is the freshest and the weather is neutral. Stand for at least 3 minutes per day gradually building up to 12 minutes. To hold this posture for prolonged periods, it is recommended that you seek professional guidance. Consistently doing Empty Standing will invigorate your Subtle Energy system. It will help to clear and organize your thinking and provide you with more restful sleep at night. Though it may seem like you did little to nothing just standing in this manner, you actually did a lot of *Qi* practice!

Western exercises can be quite invigorating for the physical body. In a like manner, Eastern Subtle Energy exercises stimulate and refresh our Energy Body. Both the short and long-term effect of these practices can increase your physical vigor and health. After practicing Empty-Standing you should notice some internal shifts. Be patient and open-minded. Listen to your body. Never force your practice. This is the way of internal study.

The Small Circle Orbit

Qi circulates in an elliptical orbit around the spine by utilizing two primary energy channels called the Conception Vessel on the front center of the body, and the Governing Vessel on the back center of the body. Both of these channels are major causeways for internal energy flow. This rotational current is the natural tidal pathway of our Qi. However, for many reasons, this flow can get restricted or blocked. Mental or physical stress, trauma, overwork, injury, poor postural or mental habits can all hamper its free movement. With some simple, gentle and intelligent undulatory posturing, you can free trapped energy, particularly around the joints, and restore the current to its natural state. Think of the movements on the following page similar to the gentle removal of debris that has fallen into a stream after a storm.

Circulating Qi
The Six Undulations

Linking the six undulations creates an elliptical energy flow around the body called the Small Circle Orbit

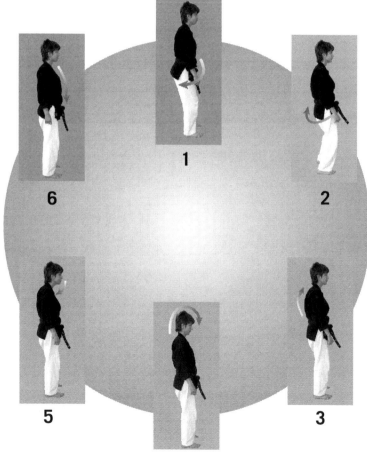

1. Tilt your pelvis back to pull Qi from the solar plexus to your perineum

2. Tuck your pelvis forward to push Qi from the perineum to your mid back

3. Sink your chest/ spread your scapula to move Qi from the mid back to base of your neck

4. Draw your head up, chin in, to pull Qi from the base of the neck to top of your palate

5. Extend your chin forward to draw chi from the upper palate to base of your throat

6. Expand you chest to draw Qi from base of the throat to your solar plexus.

PART 5
BRINGING IT DOWN TO EARTH

Heaven's plan in the production of mankind is this:
that they who are first informed should instruct those who are later in being informed,
and they who first apprehend the principles should instruct those who are slower to do so.

Menscius

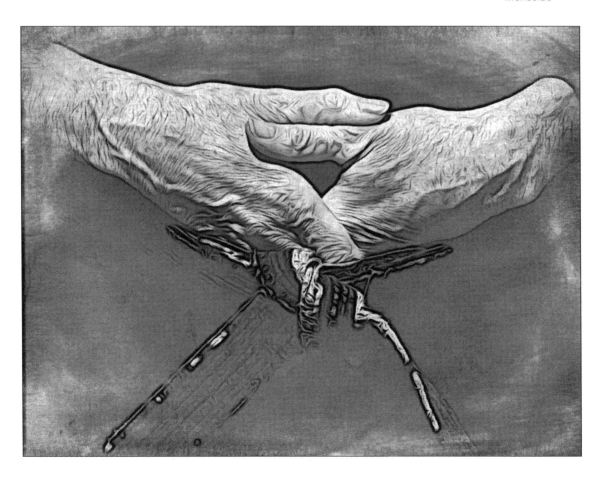

TRICK OR CHI?

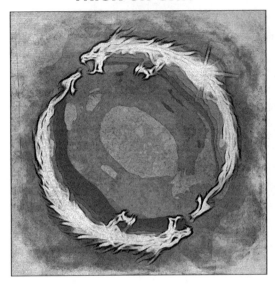

Eavesdropping On The Experts

While concluding the final chapters for this book I had started a dialog with an accomplished Goju master in the U.K., Sensei Tom Hill. Our conversations led to a lively debate about the elusive nature of *chi* in martial applications. As much as Tom wanted to believe that chi was the mystical or mystifying force behind some of the physical events he had witnessed or, in many cases, had directly experienced, he was able to find a rational explanation either in biomechanics (i.e., a barely distinguishable shift in angle) or in the mental arena as a form of suggestion or auto-suggestion. Sensei Hill's curiosity raises the larger question of how far one can go with the martial arts.

I agreed with him. There are many teachers mislabeling chi for complex torque maneuvers or simple powers of suggestion. But it has been my experience that the mind and body use unique conduits to carry both intention and physical forces to a conclusion, which I believe the Chinese, in an attempt to pin a label on it called it *Chi*. So I felt that our mutual search for truth was passionately defining the two perspectives of the half-filled, half-empty glass. Either way, like two partially blind men trying to describe the essence of a mammoth martial elephant, we both got results.

The idea struck me that this dialog ought to be part of this book. After all, isn't this the quintessential debate—the potential of the martial arts and how to make sense out of its complexities? How far can the arts *really* take us? In the end do the martial arts just boil down to an empirical combative science or are there truly transcendental truths and higher pathways embedded within these traditional disciplines? Ultimately, each of us will have to discover the answers for ourselves. I know where I stand. And I know my experience is only one frame of reference. I also know that perspectives on this subject are as varied as the human fingerprint and that the strongest will and tightest logic tends to shape the thinking of a community.

I also put the question of 'Trick or Chi' to a serious group of *yudansha* in my circle to get their candid thoughts on the merits of internal martial study, considering they had all spent at least ten years on both sides of the Hard/Soft fence. Did they think chi was a valuable asset or wishful thinking? I could not pass up the opportunity to hear their comments, for each of them had from 25-60 years experience in their respective arts. They tell it like it is. At the very least you must marvel at their diverse responses. I'll begin with the dialog that started the 'Trick or Chi' debate rolling and then present the opinions of ten senior Karateka on the subject.

Tom Hill, (40 years experience)

I am sure chi is real. But I am unsure of its physical manifestations in strength and applications other than healing.

Very few people in England seem to be talking about the subject. Most martial practitioners are in the "bash 'em" category. The Chinese claim to use it but everything I have seen is simple body dynamics and can be replicated by almost anyone once they know the trick. We have a Shaolin theatre act, which I have seen – it's been around the world. But even these guys are just using clever tricks. We have a popular kung fu teacher over here and even though he is a great practitioner and he tried to prove his chi powers to me (by lengthening his arm!) it was, in the end, a simple trick too laughable to repeat.

I have little problem, for instance, in generating power in my arm or in many other techniques. I seldom struggle with any other martial artists (with a few notable exceptions) and I have met a

lot. I can generally overcome most of their strength techniques; holds etc. even on much bigger opponents, but I put this down to technique and body dynamics rather than chi. I have even held off Chinese practitioners who claim to be using chi yet cannot make it work on me. These simple tricks or body dynamics can appear baffling if you do not know the answer.

I have yet to manifest any (other than healing) tangible effects of chi. So please do not consider my following points to be derogatory. I am merely blundering around in the dark again.

A few years back a guy who was claiming to be a Kinesiologist got a student to hold his arms out crucifix style and tested the strength of one arm with a single finger. He found it strong as he applied pressure. He then claimed he was going to affect the man's energy. He did a little routine. The next time he tried, he showed it was very easy to push the same, previously strong arm, downward.

I asked him to do the same thing with me (doubting Thomas). He achieved the same result, and claimed he was affecting my energy, but I knew what he was doing. It had to do with a minimal angle shift, hardly noticeable. But I can now replicate that result and actually teach it. It is an angle that is hardly perceivable and unless you know the trick it would be very hard to understand what was happening to your strength/energy. I am fairly sure the guy thought it was a genuine result. I don't think he was conscious of what he was actually doing. I don't think he was being dishonest. He had just subconsciously fooled himself. How do you know the same thing is not happening when a student experiences an energy loss from a supposed chi-influenced move? [Consider] Four factors:

Suggestion - the idea is planted that there will be an energy loss.

Minimal angle shift -the tiniest body dynamic shift/angle has major implications for strength.

Group consciousness - operating as a group and wishing to replicate the outcome.

Peer pressure - not wishing to be the odd one out, wishing to comply.

I suggest that some of these powerful factors need to be eliminated to establish whether chi or something else is behind these outcomes.

Sorry to be the eternal skeptic. I would love to manifest chi in training in a way that was devoid of any other external forces. I have experienced what you are talking about with Paul [a martial associate] as previously mentioned, so I am not without a degree of hope that this is achievable. Any more help would be greatly appreciated and I hope you will forgive my questioning nature as all your points are important, fascinating, worthwhile and of great interest.

Sensei Hill's healthy skepticism sets the ball rolling for the lively debate to follow.

PART 5

Author, (45 years experience)

During my first twenty-three years of training and professional teaching career I had little awareness of or interest in the concept or actuality of chi. It was not part of my training or teaching routine. None of my sensei ever seriously brought the subject up. My thoughts about the topic were basically ambivalent. Classes ran just fine. Then, one day, a single event changed my entire mindset and flung open a doorway to over twenty years of study on the subject. Since then I have conducted thousands of physical strength experiments on both lay and martial subjects. I've had the same tested on myself. We challenged ourselves to prove that our results were not a trick, particularly a leveraging principle, only to discover greater depth to this subject. We have found a few individuals seemingly immune to its effects (a truism of pressure point strikes as well. Some people simply do not respond to them) but this again opened up more intriguing observations and hypothesis. By the way, we do not tout ourselves as special. We do not flaunt our experiences. We do not advertise these insights or abilities to our junior students. We are not levitating or sending people flying through the air. We *are* elevating our martial technique. Study of this subject is by invitation only and *shodan* (first degree black belt) is the minimum requirement to participate. We want students to have a strong understanding of the body's biomechanical principles first before tackling its energetic properties. We do not care if the dojo down the street flashes esoteric knowledge on a neon billboard in front of their school or teach it to their four year olds. We are serious about our study and we have gathered a lot of strong minds behind it. My answer to the Trick or Chi question, in regards to the studies we have undertaken, is a resolute *"Chi!"*

Just as you [sensei Hill] have indicated a sensitivity to picking up 'energy' around other's bodies when doing healings, I too can often detect subtle shifts of mental energy as students adjust their body's energy fields during testing, including shifts of my own mental field responding to their changes.

I can rule out self-suggested angle shifts on my part because we have looked specifically at this factor. We describe technique that uses subtle angle shifting as 'complex torque'.

In the world of energy vibration, dense matter is no different in its vibratory reality than fine or (psychic) vibration. In this sense, the body/mind/energy trinity has been likened to ice/water/steam. That which takes place in one vibratory field will manifest simultaneously in another. Only the rate of manifestation differs, not the information contained within it. This concept is important to understand because all three dimensions are *always* influenced in any chi versus trick test or engagement and require their mediumship for chi to exist at all in human endeavor. To the best of our comprehensions we have been intensely studying the mechanisms altering and affecting these dimensions. I have a strong analytical mind, healthy skepticism, and a great supportive team to keep our research on the up and up. We don't simply accept things at face value.

There are many methods for altering, draining, or increasing ours or another's strength but they fall into specific methodologies. As indicated earlier in this book, we distinguish seven distinct layers to any executed technique. An experience I had several years ago illustrates how a single technique can be approached from completely unique angles.

The Ninja And The Unbendable Arm

In the summer of 2010 I was introduced to an accomplished *ninjitsu* expert named Jacob. Jacob was well versed in several martial disciplines. Over the years Jacob's training had gravitated toward a hard scientific approach to the arts. He aligned with the biomechanical discoveries of the S.P.E.A.R. method (Spontaneous Protection Enabling Accelerated Response) and was eager to share some of its key points. He told me, for example, if my arm was to be seized, the SPEAR method taught that I could prevent its bending by opening my hand and extending my fingers versus what might be someone's first instinct, balling their hand into a fist. I agreed to his test. He told me to resist his attempt to collapse my arm with my hand in a fist. I was unable to counter his force. My arm folded. He asked me to do it again with an open hand. I was significantly stronger. He could not bend me. However, I asked Jacob if we could redo the experiment with my hand in a fist again. This time I moved energy from my lower dantien into my arm. My arm would not budge to his pressure no matter how hard he tried. He wanted to know what I had done to achieve my strength increase. I replied that although his scientific approach worked effectively to bend my arm, there exists other alternative, internal principles that could counter the 'scientifically proven'.

It is easy to want to rationalize that things work by one clear, exclusive method but there are many ways to skin the cat. Even the best psychologists don't fully comprehend the complexities of the human mind and the best physicists don't fully comprehend the entirety of the workings of nature. I do not think we are really trying to resolve the issue of 'Trick or Chi' or 'my way versus your way' so much as seeking the answers to what makes things work well on deep levels. We should not be surprised to find that the 'how' and 'why' of many martial techniques can be accomplished in multiple ways.

Arakawa Tenshin, (55 years experience)

A casual observer might conclude that martial technique is only enhanced by speed and power, and nothing more. It is true that the breaking of boards and cinder blocks, for example, are enhanced mostly through 'Trickery'; that is, it does not often take much Energy to break these objects; but it does take a certain amount of energy to execute even a simple break. In fact, many of the spectacular feats you have witnessed at Martial Arts tournaments were nothing more than Tricks!

However, anyone who has studied Budo for three decades, no matter what his grade or rank, must have experienced some 'freak' executions that would, at the least, raise an eyebrow on the subject of Chi or Energetic Principles.

I too have spent much time looking for answers in the realm of what the Asians refer to as *Chi, Ki, Prana* or *Kundalini*. This subject is also a curiosity amongst many levels of *Kyudansha, Yudansha, Kodansha* and Yoga practitioners alike. Yet, I find that Western practitioners of both Martial Arts and Yoga *Sadhana* are often confused about the difference between External power (*Li*) and Internal power or what the Chinese call *Jin*.

For me the question of Trick or Chi in martial application is relatively simple. Speaking strictly from the standpoint of martial science, my answer is BOTH! The martial science behind proper karate *waza* (technique) is about accuracy and fact. Whereas, when one talks purely in terms of Martial *Art*, it involves the Spiritual path of study.

However, it may not be so easy to describe chi manipulation to those who lack the proper information, perception, or the intelligence to understand the subject. In addition, there are many uninformed or biased individuals in positions of authority who skew the 'Chi or Trick' question for others

due to their own misinformation. For example, I once received a letter from someone who did not believe that Bodhidharma existed in Chinese history.

It is my belief that debates such as Trick or Chi arise today because validating information regarding chi manipulation was omitted or filtered through the centuries, especially, around the mid 1800's. For example, you will find the concepts of *Mantra, Mudra, Mandala* in virtually every method of Yoga *Sadhana*, but you will rarely find these terms in modern-day martial arts *ryu* (methods) despite the fact that these three concepts have been the nucleus for both Buddhist and Taoist Monastic methods of *Chuanfa* (Kempo).

The Ancients knew of the body's 'Electrical Travel System' and of its influence on heightening or diminishing one's own or another's physical energy.

If one is searching, the doors will eventually open to expose the information sought. Of course, one has to be ready to wedge his foot in the door to prevent its premature closing. It is ALL in the searching. Ultimately, you must make the decision what is or what is not!

White Tiger (26 years experience)

I'm reminded of this quote from Einstein, *"The closer we get to physics, the closer we get to metaphysics, the closer we get to God."* I actually think chi exists in the same way that I think God exists. Both terms describe a world most of us don't know and can't fully comprehend. Perhaps, we discover an insight that explains a portion of the incomprehensible mysteries to us. In this sense, words like 'Chi' or 'God' become one in the same, closing the gap between the known and the unknown.

I believe that some martial artists rediscover very high level body organization through their disciplines. But I ponder if through modern culture/nurture, with an over-emphasis on technology, are we actually teaching our current generation to be physically weaker, less organized and less connected to their bodies? Even though in past generations we can find consistent examples of ordinary people doing extraordinary work on a daily basis, now, when we see these people, they become famous for their mind/body skills.

One book on Anthropology cites, for example, that any primitive woman could have beaten the young Arnold Schwarzenegger in an arm wrestling match. Do we consider this chi manipulation or correct body mechanics? What's the difference? We need to clarify the variables that comprise chi.

I am less concerned about labels. I want to know what chi is made of and how we can interface with it. Given the fact that chi is 'energy' and 'energy' is everything, I tend to believe that energy/chi is an actual substance when broken down to its lowest common denominator. I believe that our chi is reawakened when our bodies relearn how to support its flow. For example, one cannot punch well with a tense deltoid, but we have to teach many karate beginners to relax their deltoids. I wonder if people a thousand years ago just naturally understood how to extend their arms without the modern vanity of feeling their own muscles.

I will continue to call some phenomenon chi. It is becoming increasingly clear to me that chi manipulation isn't ethereal or a trick. It is real. It can be cultivated. It is powerful. My goal is to become more expert working with this dynamic energy.

As to Sensei Hill, point for point.

- Regarding his Kinesiological experience, Roberto [acupuncturist], will tell you that there are horrible testers out there.
- Regarding 'suggestion' and 'group consciousness', Tom is right. It can happen. However, I've had consistent success testing people who have no clue what I'm going to do to them, never experienced martial arts, never experienced energy and never experienced kinesiological testing. (See the book; *Soul Polisher's Apprentice* love/hate paper test in Chapter 29, *Chi Wiz*)
- Sensei Hill is also right that some of these powerful factors need to be eliminated to establish whether it is chi or something else.
- Regarding his muscle testing experience, I can't tell what he means without asking him or seeing him do it.
- If Sensei Hill has mostly experienced only complex torque maneuvers, not chi, he may presume that (in martial applications) there are only parlor tricks. I have been lucky enough to experience the difference. The only distinction between us and other ardent hard style practitioners is that they haven't touched it yet in their martial art.

149

INTERNAL KARATE

Nick Armitage (27 years experience)

This topic alone could be a book-long dissertation. I feel like there are many explanations to our side of the 'Trick or Chi' debate. The most important is the extensive diversity in the testing and the character of our martial group. I believe our group is unique in the testing of our chi techniques. We are a large, diverse collection of skeptics and independent thinkers, who place our own credibility behind the years of testing we have done. No, our testing has not been a rigid scientific process but we have used due diligence and when we have found flaws in our theories we return to the drawing board. This process has brought us new and better techniques and levels of insight. A totally sterile or servo motor machine-based testing system might take out the very instrument causing the results i.e., the human element working on the human element. Using a machine is not applying a control to an experiment but a different event entirely. I do believe the use of machines could test some of our work but not in the way Sensei Hill suggests. With my engineering background I have often daydreamed on this testing process. It would be an expensive but interesting work. Lastly, what an immensely complex mechanical/energetic system we are experimenting with? Which comes first, the correct chi or the correct mechanical technique? Perhaps, this is the "***chi***cken" or the egg debate as my teacher has said—two sides of the same coin. Right chi begets right technique, begets right chi.

If someone wants to experience our techniques it would require the same diligent study we have already undertaken. I don't think much progress can be made if all is stuck in theory and discussion. It is my opinion that if Sensei Hill were to see our wide range of demonstrations he would find enough moves that he could explain through "trick" and enough he could chalk up to "haven't figured out the trick yet". A fully skeptical approach will likely lead to a skeptical outcome. *"I will look at any additional evidence to confirm the opinion to which I have already come."* (Lord Molson) To truly experience the nuances of the techniques I have seen demonstrated, I think the amount of time put into this work needs to be considered. In my experiences, with true diligence applied to the martial techniques, there is no trickery. Chi is simply part of the whole technique.

PART 5

Joe Noonan (30 years experience)

I picked up a book on Chi Kung about twenty years ago that outlined several energy meditation practices. I tried them and, as the author predicted, I became aware of internal movement after several weeks of consistent meditation. I felt previously unobserved energies flowing inside me. I understood this as my own chi, which I gradually began to control. I have since been able to consistently control other people's energies particularly during martial applications.

Everyone has Energy (chi) flowing though their body. There is no trick or magic where true chi work is involved, just a lack of understanding of how this energy functions. Mind (*Yi*) controls the chi. When we see, hear or feel external stimuli, our mind gets a signal and reacts by sending a return signal (chi) to a body part or organ to deal with it.

Every person's energy (chi) is different. One person may have a minimal or reduced flow. Another person may move or control his chi flow with dramatic results. The more you work to develop your control of chi flow the better the end result will be for whatever you are trying to accomplish. Even martial tricks will work better with better chi flow.

Tian Zhua (30 years experience)

Maybe *Tricky Chi*, because of the variety of physical, mental, and environmental factors that can affect its manifestation. As my sensitivity and discernment improved, I gained in my ability to isolate those variables, leading me to believe that chi exists and can be used to impressive effect.

The four factors that Sensei Hill offers as influencing an outcome are absolutely valid, and well-considered in my skeptical analysis of our testing. I can address each of them as they relate to my experience:

Suggestion: This was negated in our testing where there was no "expected" or "correct" outcome offered. I can honestly say that I have tested a number of techniques at Hayashi's direction with

absolutely no pre-conception as to whether a variable would result in a stronger or weaker response. Conversely, there have been a number of times where I reached a pre-conclusion on my own, only to find the result was not what I expected when tested. There were also instances where an outcome varied from Hayashi's expectations, or results experienced by my classmates, and we have been able to isolate the reason. (Often related to posture, breath, mental focus, or energetic characteristics specific to the individual. As example, I offer my own postural anomaly (I have a forward tilted neck) and my propensity to strengthen/defend myself through an inward, condensing energetic attitude, which sometimes leads to quite different results from my straight-backed, more energetically porous peers.

Minimal angle shift (what we refer to as "complex torque"): minimized by our knowledge of this valuable technique, sensitivity to its use and various testing methods to limit its impact (wrist twisting, pushing, pulling, stance tests, lifting, blocking, etc.). I believe this is further controlled by having Hayashi as a disengaged witness, as often these subtle shifts can be noted by an astute observer as well as, or better than, by the individuals performing the actions. While potentially painful to the joints, the effect of this technique on a comparative analysis can also be limited by the use of full-force testing throughout; i.e. best efforts before and after engaging chi-related variables.

Group consciousness and peer pressure: Each of the mental factors noted: suggestion, group consciousness and peer pressure, are mitigated by the fact that the individuals examining this material in our dojo are all well-seasoned, strong-willed, secure in their abilities and genuinely without any need to comply, even with their teacher, Hayashi, Shifu. I believe this group maintains a healthy skepticism without closing off possibilities. This is evidenced by the number of times the outcomes for a given individual do not conform to expectations or the results experienced by other students. Rather then feeling a need to "make it work," we have tried to analyze the variables capable of influencing an outcome until we have isolated the differentiator, and after addressing that variable, we have been able to achieve repeatable results.

As further evidence that chi may impact an outcome exclusive of the factors noted by Sensei Hill, I offer my personal experience of being strengthened or weakened from behind, with no physical contact or visual cues, as well as the results we have achieved through the use of other non-contact methods such as breath, mental posturing, and entry methods (the latter are non-contact physical movements occurring prior to engagement.)

With all of this said, based on my experience, I question whether chi has practical combat applications, given the vast conditions which can impact its effectiveness and the diverse variables presented by every individual. Perhaps, at some point, we will be better able to characterize people into energetic somatotypes, and develop "high percentage" chi techniques for a given category. Or perhaps, after enough detailed study, the energetic gestalt of a partner will emerge more clearly, and we will not need to spend so much effort on finite details; that would certainly mirror my experience working with the mechanical foundations of my Art.

At a minimum, I believe we can develop methods for enhancing our own energetic organization, strength and health. My current uncertainty regarding the combative effectiveness of chi techniques does not in any way diminish my interest in this body of study. I believe that the attentiveness demanded by this effort and the resulting increased sensitivity to the form and shifting of one's energetic organization, as well as that of others and the environment, may very well lead us to mastery of our Selves, and render physical combat inconsequential.

Tim Smith (29 years experience)

In my opinion, chi is real. It is the flow of energy created by the body. It is so natural and normal that we often take it for granted or are unaware of it. We are more likely to notice a lessening in it, as when we are sick or tired. This natural flow of energy can be enhanced for a given activity by proper physical or mental positioning.

Physical manipulation of chi involves proper aligning of the spine, the limbs, the hands and feet, even the fingers and toes, to demonstrably enhance body strength for a given task. Likewise, a physical misalignment, even one that does not seem directly related to the task at hand, can lessen the strength or power that a body can bring to bear.

Mental manipulation of chi involves *focus*--eliminating distractions and intensifying concentration on the task at hand. It involves *concentration* on the result to be attained, and it involves *conviction*. A mind firmly convinced of performing a task well will yield a superior result compared to a mind filled with doubt or disbelief in one's ability to achieve it. You will likely hit a baseball farther when

you are confident in your ability to do so. A batter who is certain to fail will not likely hit a home run.

Combining the proper bodily or mechanical alignment along with good mental concentration and a firm conviction in one's ability to attain a goal, greatly enhances performance. In the West we call this the product of sound training or good athletic ability. In Eastern terms, the result might be related to Chi Kung practices.

Simple tests show us the benefit of physical manipulation. One would not try to lift a heavy weight with bad body mechanics, sprint while holding the leg muscles tight, or swing a bat with the hands reversed. Similar tests show us the benefit of mental manipulation (i.e., of holding proper mental attitudes). Athletes commonly use visualization, or imagine performing the task well prior to attempting it, to achieve a good result.

In these terms, controlling one's own chi, or flow of energy, does not seem controversial. Although harder to accomplish, influencing another's flow of energy is also possible as chi flows between people. Just look at how the spoken word can affect another or how we obtain different results using encouragement versus criticism.

I have experienced positioning of stances and minor changes in the way one engages with another demonstrable, repeatable effects on the outcome of the interaction. Some of this is obviously mechanical, a change in the angle of torque, for instance. Other changes have no direct mechanical effect yet nevertheless provide a marked, verifiable change in the outcome. These changes cannot readily be accounted for in purely mechanical terms.

Mental, or subtle, gating can also influence another's flow of chi. Chi can be seen to flow along certain pathways. Imagining or intending the enhancement or disruption of that flow can add to or weaken the opponent's ability to throw a full force punch, resist uprooting in a stance, or resist a joint lock. Not telling the partner what one intends is a way to avoid influencing the outcome of the gating.

The Subtle Energy Body, is real. We all know people who fill up a room with their presence. This is an energetic effect, not caused by one's size or physical presence alone. We also know that one who is withdrawn, sick, or depressed seems diminished. Again, this is not a change in one's physical body but in projected energy. It is this energy or Subtle Body that we seek to affect when using mental 'actions' to influence an opponent.

Greater sensitivity to our Energy Body can be cultivated through repetition and practice in the same way that a still or quiet mind develops through meditation.

I do agree that the concept of chi is elusive. It can be difficult to define, let alone share as a common experience. This difficulty can lead to the dismissal of a demonstration of "chi" as a mere trick or, at most, a mislabeling of a more concrete rationale for an observed result. However, the interaction between two people can sometimes be explained only at the energetic level, that is, through the effect of chi.

The difficulty in perceiving chi and the ability to mistake an energetic effect with one that has a purely mechanical explanation can lead to rejecting chi as a legitimate explanation for an observed effect. However, my direct experience of the consistent replication of results has led me to accept chi as a valid explanation for the effectiveness of certain martial techniques. It has also formed a fruitful basis for the most intriguing areas of my advanced martial study.

Roberto Andrade (25 years experience)

Qi is not etheric. I work with Qi concretely on a daily basis as an acupuncturist. I consider myself manipulating an actual physical force phenomena to produce healing results. My clients don't feel lightning course through their veins, levitate off the table, or experience waves of energy flowing around their body. Typically, my patients don't feel anything at all because 1) they don't know what they are supposed to be looking for, 2) they don't care as long as they feel better. They *will* feel relief in their bodies, muscles relaxing, stress melting off, or their stuffy nose going away, etc.

My main diagnostic tool is muscle testing (clinical kinesiology). I agree that the vast majority of people who claim to practice muscle testing are not doing it correctly. A skewed application of this biomechanic can easily yield mixed results. For example, a subconscious agenda such as, "I want the arm to go weak," so I subconsciously pull the arm away from the joint slightly as I push down, or a conscious ploy by a poor practitioner who preys on "believers" to increase profitability, can skew results. A true muscle test isn't really a "muscle" test at all. It is actually an Autonomic Nervous System stability test. The strength test that Sensei Hill refers to is a test for muscular strength, which can easily be turned into a parlor trick. The two common ways of screwing it up are; 1) you pull the

arm out of the joint slightly while you push down on it (this is a common mistake martial artists make when learning muscle testing because we instinctively want to pull the person's arm towards us, and 2) pushing down on the person's arm with your own arm strength. Both test muscular/joint strength, which can harm the person being tested. There is a proper way to test with proper biomechanics and you are just going to have to seek out a good practitioner in order to learn it because, like any technique, it takes a long time to get it down. However, once you do, there is no doubt sensing when there is instability or not in the arm, eliminating any question of trick or not. Because this type of testing reads off of the nervous system (an electromagnetic system), it can be affected by Qi manipulation of the person being tested. Since Qi is a concrete phenomenon, these tests are highly reproducible with the same result. If you can't reproduce these effects, then you either need to practice more, or that's just not it.

So is Qi aether, electricity, magnetism, or hypnotism? Most people who ask this question have not been taught about Qi in a correct and concrete manner. They are confused because they look at the physical realm from a Newtonian or even Quantum Physics point of view. This is like looking at the ripples on the pond rather than the pebble thrown in. Did you know that aether was accepted as a legitimate energetic state until the time of Einstein's popularity? However, in the interest of keeping things simple, I can say that, like light, Qi has some electrical as well as magnetic properties and because of this, one could label it as Bio-electromagnetism but it's more complicated than that. The human body is dramatically affected by magnetic, electrical, and electromagnetic fields. Walk around for a day with a magnet on your forehead and see how you feel.

The search for a martial manifestation of Qi stripped of correct body mechanics is not a realistic one. I have seen (and demonstrated) many instances in which Qi is manipulated using thought and intent, without any assistance from body mechanics. However, these were all done for healing purposes, not a show of martial strength. I have seen countless martial manifestations of Qi, but all need the use of proper body mechanics. If the body mechanics aren't there, then you can liken the effect of trying to push steam through pipes that aren't aligned or connected. Or pipes which are aligned, but lack enough pressure to push the steam along. Or there may be sufficient pressure and the pipes are aligned, but there is no motive force behind the steam to guide it out. You cannot strip away the body mechanics in order to have a powerful martial demonstration of Qi force. It just doesn't work that way.

One must also note a practitioner's proprioceptive abilities. Proprioception is the ability to sense 3-dimensionality, i.e., it is the sense of oneself in 3-dimensional space. This includes sensing other objects, people, etc. Proprioception is very important because if you cannot sense it, you cannot move it. Building proprioception takes time and practice, but can be learned by anyone. Being able to sense an object (or person, organ, etc) without "physically" touching it with your fingers means you are breaking down the nature of how you view the world and your interactions with it. Now, one realizes even the way things are placed in a room becomes important. Once your proprioceptive sense is developed, Qi no longer becomes a 'maybe it is real/maybe it is not real' sort of phenomenon. You will see it as an actual physical energy that can be dealt with in scientific and concrete terms. Ancient Daoists may have seemed mystical, but they were really scientists dealing with real physical issues, learning as much as they could about how the world works through natural means. The difference is that their sense of proprioception was completely turned on (and their world wasn't as toxic.)

Aston Hugh (60 years experience)

In the spirit of the old world Asian masters, Aston, who has had a broad range of both Hard and Soft martial experiences, passed on offering his direct commentary on the subject of 'Trick or Chi'. Aston has been practicing and teaching martial arts for six decades. At 74 years old he appears strong and vital. He attributes much of his well-being to managing his energy flow. Aston feels people can get too overly intellectual about their martial arts and thus miss the wisdom inherent in centered movement. "It's all about *working it*," he says. "You've just got to do it and feel it." For Aston there is no debate. You are either in the flow or not.

INTERNAL KARATE

Priming Stances, Strikes, Blocks And Locks With Internal Power

When it gets down to it we want reliable and practical tools readily at hand for the task. Basic techniques fulfill that need and form the backbone of *every* martial curriculum. Basics are the bread and butter of the defender, the competitor, and the lifetime warrior. The Okinawans call their basics *kihon*. The *kanji* (calligraphy) for the word *kihon* has no reference to the word *Ki (qi)* at all, but it's a strange coincidence that the English spelling does. I've often thought of this innocent labeling as a cosmic play-on-words that demonstrates both the obvious and the hidden levels to martial technique.

The tangible musculoskeletal fundamentals of martial systems can be placed into four broad technical categories: **Stances/Footwork, Blocks/Parrys, Strikes, Holds/Locks.** Each category has many subdivisions.

158

This chapter will briefly examine some of the internal components of three primary techniques: the powerful, universal, leg-strengthening posture called the Horse stance; an effective arm strike called the three-quarter or vertical punch; and the torso-protective, forearm middle block. Applying internal energy principles to these techniques will magnify their power. Internal work can be as deep and as complex as you can handle.

Why Traditional Asian Technique And Kata Appear Stylized To Westerners

Martial arts in the United States are undergoing a radical transformation. New training perspectives such as the popular Mixed Martial Arts (MMA) have been challenging the efficacies of traditional methods of practice. As a traditionalist myself, I think it is important to address some of the reasons for confusion and or skepticism about the traditional arts. Many a novice encountering authentic Asian martial technique for the first time have reflected, "This is certainly different." I myself can recall being taught the *neko dachi* (cat stance) and thinking, "Who would ever fight using this awkward stance?" I've since grown a deep appreciation for the posture. But not every novice is so open-minded. One young man seeking entry into Law Enforcement after college flatly told me that the Cat stance was "ridiculous." He wasn't going to do it. Western cultures emphasize independence and non-ritualized action. We pride ourselves on our ingenuity, self-reliance, speed, and distinctness in our endeavors. By contrast, many Eastern cultures view uniformity and ritual as the glue that holds the national spirit together. So one culture's orientation to their martial arts can be very different from another's. In the light of such distinctions we can deduce four general reasons why traditional Asian technique and their movement patterns may appear overly stylized to Westerners, thus either drawing them into, or equally repelling them away from, their study.

Technique can appear stylized because Asian internal masters recognized that precise posturing, where the margins of error for limb placement are very small, sometimes with an inch, leads not only to proper biomechanics but also to greater motive force as the result of better Qi flow into the active limbs. Western cultures are not used to thinking about physical postures and movement in this way.

Technique can appear stylized because of a blind or strict adherence to a technical standard simply because it comes from an older and assumed 'wiser' culture. This can result from a failure to understand the nature of the patterns, a misinterpretation, or just poor quality training. Bruce Lee was an outspoken critic of such "organized despair." These practitioners will often repeat one of two

INTERNAL KARATE

mantras for doing their moves a particular way as, *"that's the way I was taught. I am not challenging it,"* or *"that's the way I was taught until I see a better way."* The latter group preserves its patterns in the hopes that some day a more relevant meaning may be unlocked. Unfortunately, both reasons present students with an 'empty frame,' a style lacking substance or credibility.

Technique can appear stylized because of cultural preferences which place greater or lesser emphasis on the qualities of form, aesthetics, religious, and or spiritual values, and philosophical content.

Technique can appear stylized because a performer focuses on entertainment over practical fighting value. Consider the theatrical martial arts demonstrations of major movie action stars. Their movements are too fantastic for practical use yet, their cinematic feats have inspired thousands to enter the martial arts.

It has been my professional experience that the average martial artist today does not even clearly understand simple biomechanics; for example, how their legs mechanically support their arms, let alone grasp how Qi adds to leg strength. For example, if I stood on my toes and pushed another person standing across from me with their feet flat, shoulder width apart, what do you think would happen to each of our bodies? Will one or both of us move forward or backward? See if your answer matches the reality. The answer: both bodies, if roughly equal in weight, should move backwards. The proper stance maximizes the leveraging force of the pusher's arms.

In my opinion, when traditional martial technique is clearly understood, its expression is powerful, efficient, effective, and relevant. Part of that understanding comes from acknowledging that such techniques and their patterns have inherent internal values that have been obscured by more topical goals. The first value to be considered in the internal formula is 'structure', or what we can call body architecture.

Structure

When it comes to energy work, we consider the posturing of the whole person (physical, mental, emotional) as causing one of three general effects:

The structure/action/organization adds Qi to the physical technique

The structure/action/organization is neutral to the physical technique

The structure/action/organization subtracts Qi from the physical technique

The optimal posture/structure/action must include **three primary alignments**: the spine and limbs must maximize Qi flow to the muscles of the specified task; the mind (thought and intention) must be in accord with the outcome; the breath must be in accord with both the body motion and mental intent. When synchronized, these three components greatly magnify any martial technique.

When the Energy Body is activated unusual events can occur, as evidenced by some of the stories at the beginning of this book. Proper internal structure can sometimes be counterintuitive to obvious biomechanical logic, defying the expected results. For example, one day I was demonstrating how to uproot an advanced student from a stance by pulling him. The student asserted that one's body weight, muscular strength, and leverage were the only prime factors that pulled another person out of their stance. "You dig in, lean back and pull," he said, to which I leaned forward and pulled him right over even though he outweighed me and was leaning back against my pull. He was both baffled and excited that I had just demonstrated a non-logical technique. I explained to him that energy work was not illogical. I was simply applying logic in a training dimension he was unfamiliar with.

Qi Principles
In Martial Stances

Stance, or what the Japanese call *dachi,* simply implies a way of standing or posturing with the legs. Generations of martial artists have carefully evaluated the many ways people have withstood unbalancing agents, how our legs convey us to or away from an opponent, and how they generate torque and weight behind our techniques. The most suitable postures for combative or competitive purposes were selected for their superior attributes.

Martial legwork generally falls into two broad, classifications: stances that **stabilize** and/or stances that **mobilize**. The most stable stances are wide-based. The most mobile stances are high or narrow-based.

The *kiba dachi* or horse-riding stance is the most practiced, wide-based stance in the world. Its strength benefits are obvious. With the legs bent low, the quadreceps get a solid workout while offering tremendous resistant power against lateral forces. But there is more to this stance then its mechanical efficiencies and superb leverage. The Horse stance can lead us into a greater understanding of Qi principles inherent in all stance work.

Internally, stances define our root to the earth. Our legs form energy 'taproots,' like the two prongs of an electrical plug. Our physical feet don't actually sink into the ground to hold us any firmer. However, our Energy Body, which extends beyond our epidermis, does root us. Different stances create various groundings categorized by whether they add to rising/lifting, sinking/rooting, absorbing/transmitting, or equalizing energies. Lightening, lifting, floating, mobilizing, lowering, rooting, receiving or transmitting, even stilling, are not just physical or psychological descriptions of martial technique. They define traits of a very pliable Subtle Energy Body that has special characteristics distinctly different from the physical body. The Chinese consider the Horse stance an Earth Element posture. Though one might easily see the visual rationale for this descriptor, the Horse posture itself actually causes a specific shift in the electromagnetic fields around the body.

Every year, for over twenty years running, I have taught an introductory martial arts class to students at New Jersey's, Drew University. Early in the curriculum I present the *kiba dachi* (horse stance). I explain its basic structure and the characteristics that distinguish it from other stances; feet roughly a shoulder width and half apart, knees bent, back straight, pelvis tucked forward. Naturally, some students have a better Horse posture than others due to a more suitable anatomy. I then have them do a resistance test to demonstrate their stance's strength against a lateral push. Most students are impressed with its resistant power. If I never added another detail about this posture they would all develop substantially stronger Horse stances. But they would be missing a hidden and essential ingredient, something I intentionally left out. Every karate technique possesses both an exoteric (outer) and esoteric (inner) rationale. I give my class the exoteric fundamentals but I hold back its 'esoteric' or inner fundamentals for later study.

As a teaser, I ask the group if they think the strength of their horse stance would be affected by where they locate their mind? Do *you*, the reader, think it makes a strength difference if you were thinking about or directing your intention to your thumb, big toe, or the top of your head while you were pushed from the side in a Horse stance? Do you think it would alter the strength of your legs where you placed your mind in your body? When the students discover just how much of a difference it makes, their minds wake up.

The Internal Properties Of The Horse Stance

Chin pulled in—shoulders down—knees pressed outward—feet straight with the proper proportionality of width—pelvis tucked under the torso—belly relaxed—mentally intend downward into the ground.

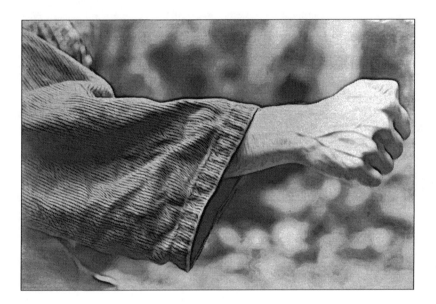

Qi Principles
In Martial Strikes

Because the martial arts have such an impressive and devastating striking inventory, its stances and parries often play second fiddle to its bone-shattering, wood-splintering hand and leg attacks. Limb strikes are simply divided into arm versus leg maneuvers with arm strikes broadly consisting of all manner of finger, knuckle, hand, elbow and forearm work, and the legs hitting with the ball, heel, blade or side of foot, shin and knee.

Some masters see blocks as a form of striking just as strikes can be considered a form of blocking, so we will consider takedowns, joint locks, and grappling techniques in this gray zone. Also, in the monastic temple arts of Asia certain striking actions, performed solo, were considered to possess more therapeutic value over other methods.

For our purposes we will look at a specific arm strike called the Three Quarter Punch. Its name is derived from the position of the fist at the end of the punch. The fist is rotated approximately three quarters, palms down, toward the thumb side. Most martial artists throw the popular karate twist or corkscrew punch, where the fist comes to rest at near full extension, often with the palms facing completely down. Instead of trying to debate the value of one style of punching over another, I have found it much more insightful to look at the merits of individual strikes. All punching methods have their unique advantages.

Internal Properties Of The Vertical Punch

The fingers are rolled and pressed into the upper portion of each finger's first joint pad—the thumb is pressed into the second joint of the index finger (different thumb positions effect different energy currents)—the knees are pressed outward prior to punching—the chin is drawn in to straighten the neck—the pelvis is tucked forward—the anal sphincter is tightened—The fist rotates to a three-quarter position on extension—the toes are pressed/splayed into the ground for the most surface coverage. There are at least four primary fist chambers noted in internal karate work.

Qi Principles
In Martial Blocks

When the martial arts blossomed in the U.S. in the 1960's many practitioners of Japanese, Okinawan, and Korean fighting styles readily embraced the logic of redirecting their opponent's strike away from their body with the use of *blocks*. The word 'block' is a misleading term that implies the direct obstruction of another's blow, rather than a redirection of its force. It wasn't until the 1990's that mainstream martial literature began presenting traditional 'blocks' as more then just deflecting moves. Blocks could readily turn into strikes or set ups for joint locks. It seems that our Western fixation on karate's superficial actions had limited these supposedly defensive actions to simple and sole redirections of an opponent's limbs.

Not only are Qi principles behind the use of blocks, but these maneuvers are not actually used by advanced practitioners as blocks at all.

Nevertheless, since countless U.S. dojos teach basic blocking drills, I have selected one variant of the middle block taught in the isshinryu system of Okinawa. To maximize any middle blocking action we will direct Qi into the arm to enhance its stopping power.

Internal Properties Of The Middle Block

The chin is pulled in—the knees are pressed outward to pump Qi upwards—elbow is held one fist away from the side—forearm is rotated ¾ to the outside —no less than a 90 degree angle of forearm to upper arm—feet are straight—pelvis is tucked inward—thumb is placed on top of the fist and pressed outwards—an equilateral triangle is formed with the upper and lower arm and the space between the fist and shoulder. The middle block has two applications, not one standard method of application. There is an *extending* middle block and a *retracting* middle block due to distinct differences in the Subtle Energy Body—the chambering of the hands is specific—There are many internal formulas to accomplish extra strength which is why we see sound technical systems packaged differently—because there is a receiving and transmitting middle blocking action, the breath must be aligned properly to facilitate the correct action.

Note On Working With Subtle Energy

The successful outcome in directing Subtle Energy into any block, strike, stance or lock relies on many factors, some of which may not be apparent without considerable training or guidance in internal energy principles. Be patient. Be open-minded. There is much to be gained investigating this unique platform of study. The Western term 'Subtle Energy Body' is just that—understated. Sensing your own fine energy flow may at first be frustratingly hard to perceive. Many students initially discover their internal energy by way of its outcomes rather then by direct sensation. Detecting such flow may at first be likened to looking for a pair of glasses on the end of your nose. Our energy body

is so close to us, so ever-present, that we fail to see it simply because we *are* it! One final note: Internal work is not a replacement for Hard style training, but a complimentary practice. Hard and Soft techniques enhance one another. The ultimate alchemy is to blend both principles.

If you do note a successful increase in speed or strength in the above techniques you stand at the threshold of a new way of looking at your martial art. In future writings I will go into greater detail about the workings of the Energy Body and its relationship to martial practice.

Let's return to our assault scenario at the beginning of Part 3. As the action unfolds see if you can more clearly identify the defender's use of the seven Gates of Power.

The Assault Revisited

On the way to your car that night you didn't see them. Now your very life is threatened. A shocking, skull-jarring blow from behind numbs your mind and buckles your legs, releasing a warm fluid that streams down your lacerated scalp. Despite a few seconds of momentary unconsciousness, your primitive reptilian brain senses hands forcefully trying to subdue your arms and switches on your millions year old fight reflex. You twist instinctively with brute, impulsive strength (Gate 2). You tear one offending arm off but another tightens. The grip is simply too strong to break. One attacker holds you as another rains ruthless fists upon your head, each more violent than the previous. You jerk backward (Gate 3) barely avoiding a sharp object brushing your face. Your assailant has a knife! The thought jolts your adrenaline system giving you enough energy to break the clutch (Gate 2). Still a relentless onslaught of fleshy tentacles tries to subdue you. You barely escape one grab by circling your arm out of it (Gate 4). Wiping a sheet of blood from your brow you count three shadowy forms. Thick-muscled arms lunge for your throat. You push back hard (Gate 2). Outweighing the shadow, it tumbles backward. A second, bigger shadow tries the same tactic. You retreat at the moment of his lunge, sending him stumbling forward. He did not expect to meet emptiness (Gate 3). For no conscious reason when he gets up to try again, instead of pushing directly into him or stepping back, you slip your arms up under his, and lift him high onto his heels (Gate 4). You sense his confusion and surprise that he cannot budge you. Undeterred, the other two shadows continue their assault.

Eighteen seconds have elapsed since your head took its first concussive blow. Having stalled one attacker your mind hits a clearing. A new resolve emerges. Survival instinct has fully kicked in from the adrenaline rushing into your bloodstream. Dilating blood vessels are now pumping raw oxygenated energy into your limbs. You stonewall the next punch with a rising forearm (Gate 4), then surprise yourself by kicking instinctively into the shadow's groin (Gate 2). He drops, writhing in pain, clutching his ruptured testicle. As if a channel had suddenly switched in your head, the reality floods in that you *are, and have been for thirty years,* a martial sensei. That first traumatizing blow had blunted your skills from consciousness. Now they spring back with a vengeance. Your trained response unleashes full force. You tuck your pelvis, coordinating the action with a deep and focused exhale. Your thumb springs on top of your rolled fingers and your legs widen to buttress your punch (Gate 5). The closest shadow never sees your piston-primed fist explode forward. It slams into his sternum snapping his sternal notch from its cartiliginous hinge and slices into his viscera. The third shadow with the knife lunges in desperation. Your moves gain fluidity as you drop into a *neko-dachi*, catch/*hiki-te*, and withdraw (Gate 5). Your breath floods into your primed energy filled dantien. Suddenly, your armed assailant experiences an immediate and pervasive body weakness (Gate 6) from the *'suck/spit'* energy technique your Okinawan sensei once taught you. Before he regains his stability you chop deep into his carotid artery, compressing it, causing a severe drop in his blood pressure (Gate 2). Disoriented and desperate to avoid falling, he grabs your arms. You seal his chest gates (Gate 6) depriving his chi from entering his upper arms then easily lock onto his wrist and torque the knife from his fingers (Gate 4). He is at your mercy. Summoning chi into your eyes you assume

the Tiger's Gaze beckoning your attackers with your palms upward to enter your iron ring of power (Gate 5). Fear-striken, one assailant turns in retreat and stumbles head long into three police officers. The muggers are collared and charged with assault and battery. You decline to press charges despite your deeply lacerated brow (Gate 7). Later you lament that being a Buddhist and remembering to show compassion to all living beings is not an easy precept to practice. For weeks after the incident you meditate (Gate 1/7), sending compassion to the three assailants hoping that they find a clearer path for their future lives and that you find safer paths home from work (Gate 7).

Unraveling The Mystery Of Power

Looking back at the twenty-two accounts of unusual phenomenon at the beginning of this book you might now have a better understanding of some of the principles behind them, the unusual ways in which power flows, and the choices you have to influence life's outcomes. Whatever you call the mysterious power behind these events; God, Universal Mind, ESP, acute sensitivity, sound body mechanics, good mind/body teamwork, Qi, or just plain luck, one thing is sure. We are plugged into more energy networks than we have been conditioned to believe. There are levels of information and energy out there for all of us with the right effort. The martial arts give us one excellent entry point. A certain amount of healthy skepticism is also a good thing. Do I really believe that Konstantin's cousin, Michale actually leapt six feet in the air onto the wall? I would have said "no way" until I saw an athlete actually jump effortlessly upon a wall *over his head*! When you consider that a panicked mother has lifted a two thousand pound car off her baby, it stirs me to wonder what are the limits of physical accomplishment. I will be the first to scrutinize such phenomena. I am not looking for extraordinary feats with my martial studies. I am looking to simply enjoy a rich and meaningful life. I've always felt that for every magic trick revealed there awaits a new magic to reawaken the awe in us. This happened to me in mid-career when I was granted a taste of the unknown and initiated into Karatedo's inner world. Those events have inspired me to chase these mysteries and I am most favorable to those who wish to join with me in the pursuit.

Hayashi Tomio
Bodhisattva Warrior Monk
Chen Yen Shingon Mikkyo Mi Ching Order
Isshin Kempo Headmaster, 8th Dan
45 years of martial arts experience

I took up Hard style karate at age seventeen. At the publishing of this book I was sixty-three. I have never stopped training and exploring my art. Since my first dojo class as a gangly neophyte at the infamous Bank Street Dojo in Summit, New Jersey, December 12, 1968, something new has always greeted my martial curiosity. I hope that you find your wonder stirred, as I have, for these rich and venerable disciplines. Internal work is a fascinating, compelling, and a fruitful field of study that can enhance anyone's martial skills and everyday Life.

I wrote this book as an introduction to a particular way of looking at martial philosophy and techniques beyond the cliched and also, with the small hope that some of this information would provide a foothold for Hard stylists unfamiliar with the internal terrain residing in their own arts. This book isn't meant to answer or clarify all curiosities and questions about the subject—far from it. It's a vast topic. I've simply taken some broad strokes to a great canvas and created a few peepholes into the magnificent rooms of the Great Martial Mansion from my own personal foray into the field. I hope this material raises more questions and urges you to probe further, the dynamic and sacred currents coursing through the martial disciplines — always within your grasp.

Check us out at **www.isshinkempo.com**
and continue the dialog

More Books By Christopher J. Goedecke
(Buddhist, Hayashi Tomio)

The Soul Polisher's Apprentice
A Martial Kumite About Personal Evolution
354 pgs., non-fiction
(Available on Amazon and Kindle)

For Young Adults
The Unbreakable Board
And The Red Dragon Surprise
89 pgs., fiction
(Available on Amazon and Kindle)

Smart Moves, A Kid's Guide To Self-Defense
Hardcover, photo essay, non-fiction

The Wind Warrior, Training Of A Karate Champion
Hardcover, photo essay, non-fiction

Find out more at
www.isshinkempo.com

52930540R00097

Made in the USA
Lexington, KY
15 June 2016